THE COMPLETE fabric artist's workshop

SUSAN STEIN

Creative Publishing international

www.creativepub.com

THE COMPLETE
fabric
artist's
workshop

SUSAN STEIN

Creative Publishing international

First published in the United States of America by
Creative Publishing international, Inc., a member of
Quayside Publishing Group
400 First Avenue North
Suite 300
Minneapolis, MN 55401
1-800-328-3895
www.creativepub.com
Visit www.Craftside.Typepad.com for a behind-the-scenes peek at our
crafty world!

ISBN-13: 978-1-58923-663-9
ISBN-10: 1-58923-663-7

10 9 8 7 6 5 4 3 2

Copy Editor: Karen Levy
Proofreader: Alissa Cyphers
Book Design: Tina R. Johnson
Cover Design: Mighty Media
Page Layout: Danielle Smith

Printed in China

Permission to reproduce the printed images from Carol Belanger Grafton,
ed., Authentic Chinese Cut-Paper Designs, Dover Design Library (New
York: Dover Publications, Inc., 1988), used in Printout to Fabric Transfer,
granted by Dover Publications, Inc.

dedication

To my dad, C. Emmett Shogren, who was my greatest supporter and encouraged me to accomplish whatever I set my mind to.

To my husband, John, for many years of love, support, and encouragement.

contents

i can do that with this?

With busy lives and lots of distractions, taking a little time out to **play**, to **create**, to find out **"what if"**– is important.

These small and portable projects make catching some creative time easy. Designed as "journal pages," they are fun to do at group get-togethers and with kids. They also require very little equipment.

The idea for making fabric journal pages began during a Quilt Market in Houston. Among all the gorgeous quilts, wall hangings, and garments were small pieces that chronicled people's lives throughout a year. Some included writing and poetry, but typically the page alone conveyed a message. It was an arresting exhibit because it was so unusual and personal. Inspired, I began to teach a journal class to explore innovative techniques for, with, and on fabric. I encouraged students to pick a theme that held meaning for them, both to express themselves and to contribute unity to their collection of pages. You'll see a haiku journal, a dragonfly-dusted wall hanging, and autumn-as-inspiration pieces in the Artists' Gallery at the back of the book.

Who knew we would paint fusible web, make beads from fabric, and take worms out of cocoons? But new ideas pop up constantly and the only thing stopping fiber artists from trying something is the desire to do it all right now!

The Complete Fabric Artist's Workshop takes you through 27 techniques that use paint, fiber, embellishments, and even copy machines to make personal pages. These can then be used for wall hangings, fabric books, matted pieces, screens large and small, boxes, and anything else your imagination can devise. You may find yourself inspired to create larger pieces that combine several of the techniques, or perhaps you'll apply the artful approaches to enhance garments.

In preparation for making the projects, collect the best paints and fabrics you can find. Prepared-for-dyeing (PFD) fabric is ideal for any painting technique; it has no sizing or finish to interfere with good paint absorption. You will find PFD fabrics at fine quilt shops. For all of the projects, you will want to start with pieces of fabric cut at least 9" x 11½" (22.9 x 29.2 cm) so you have a little "insurance" while working or for seam allowances. After you complete a piece, you can trim it to the finished book size, 8½" x 11" (21.6 x 27.9 cm), unless you plan to mat it or sew it onto another piece of fabric.

I used paints by Jacquard for many of the methods in *The Complete Fabric Artist's Workshop*. They layer well and offer a range of possibilities: Dye-na-Flow,® a thin transparent paint, behaves almost like a dye; Textile Colors,® a medium-bodied paint, also gives transparent coverage; Neopaque® colors are opaque; and Lumiere® colors are metallic. Embellishments I found everywhere—even at the hardware store!

The makers of some of the products used with certain techniques never intended (or imagined) such uses, so be prepared for unexpected results! Many techniques should be tried a couple of times before using them to make a final project piece. Write notes with a permanent marker on the edges of practice pieces to record what you did. Turn a mistake into a happy accident whenever you can.

Keep a file of test samples (and articles and resources) so you can easily find them when you want them. Be mindful of safety precautions when using products like bleach or when melting synthetic materials; work outside when possible or work in a vented room. Most of all, cultivate a playful attitude and be ready for the question *"How* did you DO that?"

Susan L. Stein

COLOR
and
IMAGERY

paintstiks technique quartet

Artists have used paintstiks—linseed oil and pigment solidified into a stick form—for many years.

Versatile, easy to use, and permanent when set properly, they come in many colors and a wonderful array of iridescent hues. A blender stick—a colorless stick used for making value gradations—allows you to create lighter colors. You can purchase paintstiks individually or in sets.

Now that the fiber people have discovered them, paintstiks have become a very popular tool for decorating clothing, wall hangings, cloth books, and art dolls.

Apply the color directly to the fabric—it's just like coloring with a crayon. You can use paintstiks to make rubbings of fairly flat objects that have recesses deep enough to feel through fabric, or try one of the many commercial rubbing plates. Stencil using a stencil brush and any purchased stencil design (or make your own stencil from freezer paper or template plastic). Use masking-tape guides to paint straight lines for plaids. Pull the color off of a paper with torn edges to create lovely, soft stripes.

Clean hands and brushes with citrus cleaner, workshop solvent, or soap and water. Protect your carpet and your clothing, as any flakes of paint that fall from your work surface will dry and become a permanent stain.

materials and tools

Plastic cover for the table

Nonslip surface: Grip-n-Grip

Masking tape

Fabric: washed and ironed to remove sizing and wrinkles

Paintstiks:
Shiva Artist's Paintstik

Paper towels

Small knife

Rubbing plates

Stencils

Bristle stencil brushes:
¼" (6 mm) or ½" (1.3 cm)

Iron

Cooking parchment
(available at grocery stores)

Kraft paper

Cardstock

Double-stick tape

paintstiks technique quartet

Use your quartet of techniques in a variety of ways— try each as a stand-alone device or combine two or more paintstik techniques in one composition.

Preparation

Protect your work surface with the plastic cover. Before you begin, read through all of the techniques described in this section. One technique may contain a detailed instruction that is necessary for related techniques.

Write or Draw

Place the nonslip surface on your table. Using masking tape, adhere three edges of the fabric to the surface, right side up. Peel off the protective skin that forms on the outside of the paintstik, either by pinching it off with a paper towel or trimming it off with a small knife. When the stick glides easily over a piece of paper, it is ready to use. Write words or draw abstract lines on the fabric with the paintstik.

Note: If the paintstik wears down to the cardboard cover, loosen the cover around the stick and push the stick up from the opposite end, leaving the cardboard intact.

Make a Rubbing

Slide a rubbing plate under the fabric through the open edge. Stroke over the fabric with the flat end of the paintstik to capture the pattern from the rubbing plate. Move the plate as needed and continue to stroke the paint onto the fabric. You can use more than one color if you like, but be careful not to smudge already painted areas. You will, with a little practice, be able to avoid stroking off the edges of the rubbing plate.

Stencil

Tape a stencil to the fabric or hold it firmly in place. Choose a brush size appropriate to the stencil openings. To smoothly load your stencil brush with paint, first stick a large piece of masking tape to your work surface, then rub the paintstik onto the back of the tape. Load the brush by picking up as much paint as possible from the tape. Brush the color from the stencil edge into the opening to create a soft outline that lightens toward the motif center.

Note: You can create a stencil from freezer paper! Cut out a shape, leaving approximately 2" (5.1 cm) of paper as a surround. Iron the paper, shiny side down, directly onto the right side of the fabric.

Create Soft Forms

Tear strips of cardstock. Apply double-stick tape to the back of the strips, and place them on the fabric where you want to create a stripe. Stroke a paintstik onto the paper and then brush the paint from the torn paper edge onto the fabric to make a soft stripe. Repeat for as many stripes as desired. To mix colors, apply your paintstiks to a large piece of masking tape or rough paper and then mix the paints with your brush.

Finishing

Let the fabric dry for at least two to three days. If you try to work with it earlier, the paint will smear. Set an iron to the correct temperature for the type of fabric you are using. Protect your ironing surface with a piece of parchment or kraft paper. Iron the back of each area for 10 to 15 seconds.

Susan Suggests

To give an appliqué a three-dimensional effect, draw around it with a paintstik to create a shadow.

paintstik decorated apron

Use oil paint sticks and a rubbing plate to decorate a butcher apron with a colorful design.

Shiva Artist's Paintstiks come in many colors and are easy to use. Once they dry and are properly heat set, the color is permanent. Choose matte or iridescent colors, apply them easily, and iron to set the color.

materials and tools

plastic cover for the table

apron fabric: ⅞ yd. (0.8 m) pant-weight cotton

iron

scissors

nonslip sheet: Grip-n-Grip

rubbing plates

paintstiks: assorted colors

paper towels or small knife

cooking parchment (available at grocery stores)

bias tape: one package (3 yd. [2.75 m]) wide double-fold

pins

thread: to match apron and bias tape

sewing machine

heavy cardboard

craft knife

glue for cardboard

paint for cardboard: house paint, textile paint, or acrylic

paintstik decorated apron

Preparation

Cover your work surface with plastic. Protect your carpet and clothing, because any flakes of paint that fall from the work surface will dry and become a permanent stain.

1

Rinse the apron fabric to preshrink it and remove sizing and wrinkles. Press. Enlarge the pattern on page 49 and use it to cut out the apron.

2

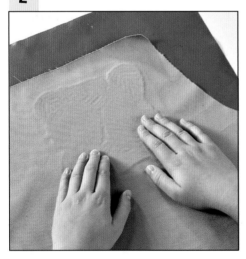

Place the nonslip sheet on the table. Choose one or more rubbing plates and arrange them on the sheet. Cover the plates with the apron faceup. Use your hands to press the apron onto the rubbing plate so you can tell where the edges of the design are located.

3

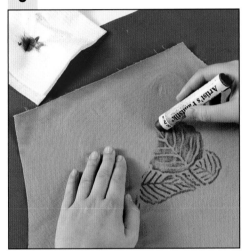

Peel off the protective skin that forms on the flat end of the paintstik, either by pinching it off with a paper towel or trimming it off with a small knife. Carefully dispose of the peelings so they don't get on your clothes or floor. Place your left hand firmly down on the left side of the area of the apron to be decorated to hold it in place. Rub over the area covering the rubbing plates with the paintstik, trying not to go beyond the edges of the raised designs and stroking in one direction, away from your left hand. (Or switch hands and directions if you are left-handed.) Let the apron dry undisturbed for two to three days, depending on how heavily the paintstik was applied.

4

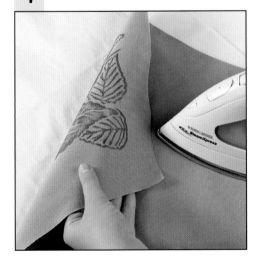

Protect your ironing surface with cooking parchment. Place the apron facedown and iron with a dry iron for 10 to15 seconds in each spot that was decorated. Make sure the room is well ventilated. This will make the paint permanent to washing, but the apron (or any project colored with paintstiks) should not be dry-cleaned.

Continued

5

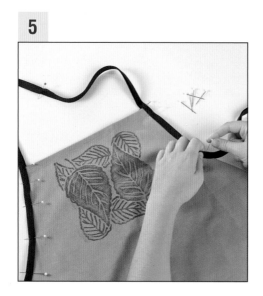

Turn under the top edge, long sides, and bottom edge of the apron ¼" (6 mm); press. Turn under ½" (1.3 cm) again; press and stitch. Fold the bias tape in half to determine the center. Place the tape around your neck so the center mark is in back and mark the tape where you want the top edge of your apron. Pin the bias tape around the remaining raw edges of the apron, with the wider fold on the back of the apron. Align the marks with the top edge, creating a neck strap, and extend the ends beyond the sides to make ties. Sewing from the right side, stitch the tape along the full length.

Custom Rubbing Plates

To make your own rubbing plates, start with a large square of cardboard and then cut a design out of a second piece of cardboard, using a craft knife. Glue the design to the square, weight it down with books, and let dry. Or glue string or kids' letters to the cardboard. Paint the entire surface of the cardboard to seal it and let dry. Use as a rubbing plate as described in step 3. Other household items, such as trivets, can also be used as rubbing plates.

Susan Suggests

Paintstiks are the perfect medium to grab for embellishing a project that needs a little spark, such as a wall hanging with a plain border or an ordinary sweatshirt cut up the front to make it a unique jacket.

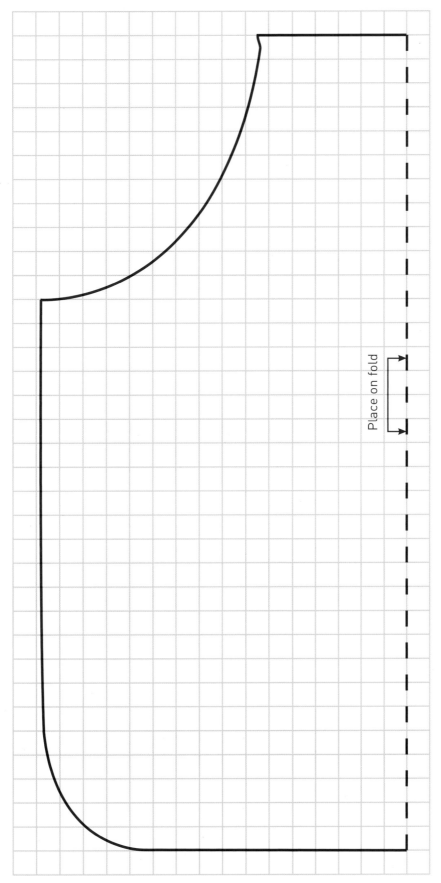

Place on fold

1 square = 1" (2.5 cm)

brayer painting

Brayers are like small versions of the rollers used to paint walls.

They are very useful for applying paint to fabric in a variety of ways—each one interesting and fun! You can create patterns by placing items around the roller before loading it with the paint. Brayers with a removable roller make it easy to wind threads and fibers around the roller. Create a different effect by putting objects under your fabric and rolling a paint-filled brayer over the top.

Creating garment fabric with abstract designs is easy, as the brayer covers a large area quickly. It is simple to create fascinating texture with common household items. Mix the techniques for a variety of looks. Let's get started!

materials and tools

Plastic cover for the table

Medium-bodied fabric paint: Lumiere or Neopaque, assorted colors

Glass with taped edges or an acrylic surface

Soft rubber brayer (not sponge) with a removable roller

Fabric

Masking tape

Iron

Objects for texture: rubbing plates, bamboo placemats, cheesecloth, produce bags, bubble wrap, leaves, plastic doilies, or scrapbook-type corrugated cardboard

String or rubber bands

brayer painting

Build the techniques one over another on the same fabric, or use separately.

Preparation

Protect your work surface with the plastic cover. Before you begin, read through all of the techniques described in this section. One technique may contain a detailed instruction that is necessary for related techniques.

Load the Brayer

Pour a puddle of paint onto part of a sheet of glass or acrylic. Roll the brayer over the paint to spread it into an even layer. Roll the brayer on a clean spot on the glass, in one direction, to flatten any thick paint and evenly distribute paint around the roller. Press lightly when moving the roller.

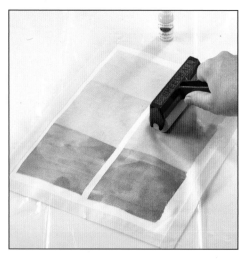

Fashion a Plaid Pattern

Attach your fabric to the table with masking tape. Roll the paint-loaded brayer down a section of fabric to create a line. Note that every revolution of the roller removes a layer of paint from the brayer, so the color lightens rapidly across the fabric. Apply more paint to the brayer and paint another line. Load the brayer with a second color (no need to clean it), and roll over the fabric, perpendicular to the already painted lines, to create your plaid. The end result will be an interesting composition, depending on how quickly the roller runs out of paint, where the painted areas overlap, how evenly you loaded the brayer, and how smooth the plastic is under the fabric. Press to heat set the paint.

Work with Texture

Place your chosen texture object or objects under a piece of fabric. Roll over the top of the fabric with a loaded brayer. Reload the brayer when it runs out of paint. Notice how the roller will create a negative image when you go beyond the edge of the item underneath the fabric. Press to heat set the paint.

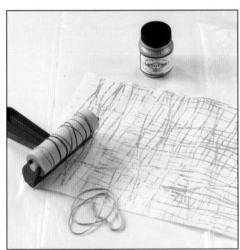

Design Stripes and Grids

Prepare an even layer of paint on the glass or acrylic. Clean the brayer. Remove the roller. Wind string or fibers around it or place rubber bands of varying widths on it. Replace the roller in the brayer and load it with paint. Roll over the fabric, either making irregular stripes by going in one direction or a grid by going in both directions. Press to heat set the paint.

Note: The paint on the glass or acrylic must be evenly rolled out so paint does not move into the spaces between the string or rubber bands.

Susan Suggests

Scatter rubber bands under a piece of fabric for an interesting abstract effect.

brayer-painted lunch bag

If your idea of packing a lunch is to throw a beverage and a frozen entrée into your briefcase, here's a great idea for you!

This attractive, insulated lunch bag is also a conversation-starter at work or on the bus! Brayer painting over textured items makes a unique fabric for the outside layer. A dense quilt batting provides the insulation, and a tightly woven cotton lining resists snags from silverware. Make lunch bags for the kids too, using their plastic letters and other toys for rubbing patterns. Better yet, have them make their own bags!

materials and tools

- plastic cover for the table
- rotary cutter, acrylic ruler, and mat
- outer fabric: ½ yd. (0.5 m)
- batting: 12" x 32" (30.5 x 81 cm), fusible cotton/polyester by Hobbs
- ½ yd. (0.5 m) of cotton fabric (such as batik)
- textured items: rubbing plates, bamboo placemats, plastic lace, kids' letters, leaves, etc.
- tape: double-stick and masking
- paint: Neopaque or Lumiere by Jacquard
- large plastic plate or a piece of template plastic or glass for rolling out paint
- soft rubber brayer (available at craft and art supply stores)
- iron
- sewing machine with zigzag stitch
- thread
- Velcro: 3" (7.5 cm)

brayer-painted lunch bag

Preparation

Cover your work surface with plastic.

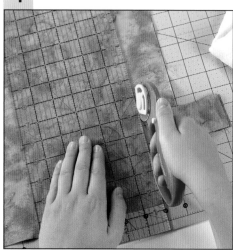

With a rotary cutter, ruler, and mat, measure and cut 12" x 32" (30.5 x 81 cm) pieces of outer fabric, batting, and lining fabric.

Lay out textured items on the plastic-covered table so they cover a 12" x 32" (30.5 x 81 cm) area. Use double-stick tape to hold them in place.

3

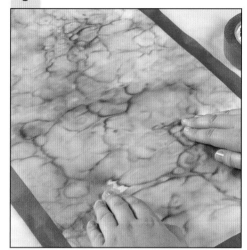

Place the outer fabric over the textured items and tape the edges to the plastic-covered table, using masking tape. Rub your fingers over the fabric so you can make a slight imprint where the rubbing materials are located.

4

Pour paint onto the glass or plastic palette, and roll the brayer through it until there is paint evenly distributed around the roller in a thin layer.

Continued

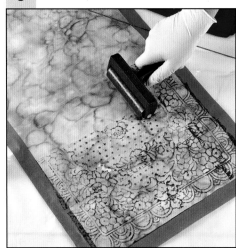

Working quickly so the paint doesn't dry, roll over the fabric in the shorter direction, reloading the brayer for every pass. Let the paint dry. Iron the fabric on the back with a dry iron to set the paint.

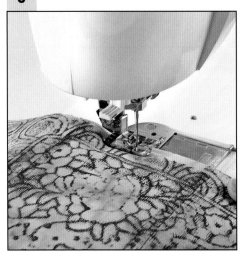

Layer the outer fabric, batting, and lining. Fuse the layers together by steaming, first from one side and then from the other side. Follow the batting manufacturer's directions. Set your machine for a fairly wide satin stitch and sew all around the edges of the quilt sandwich.

7

Fold the quilt sandwich in half, right sides together, aligning the short ends. The short ends will become the top of the bag. Stitch the sides with a ¼" (6 mm) seam.To make gussets at the bottom, flatten the bottom, forming triangles on each side, with the side seams centered in the triangles. Sew across each triangle, perpendicular to the seam, 2" (5 cm) from the point.

8

Turn the bag right side out. Center a piece of Velcro loop tape along the top edge of one side; stitch it in place. From the opposite side, fold down both sides of the upper edge twice, 1½" (3.8 cm). Mark where the hook tape should be. Unfold the bag and stitch the hook tape to the outside of the bag.

Susan Suggests

Practice loading and using the brayer before starting your project. It is difficult to get an entirely even application of the paint because the brayer puts down more paint on the first revolution of the roller, but putting too much paint on will blur the rubbing completely.

quilted/painted folder briefcase

Set yourself apart as a creative, interesting, yet professional, person at your next committee meeting.

Sized to hold several file folders, this tote will have them wondering how you made such a unique fabric. Simple quilting, and then painting afterward, creates a wonderful texture and pattern.

Try small samples of different combinations. If you like them all, make a tote for every organization you belong to!

materials and tools

plastic cover for the table

rotary cutter, acrylic ruler, and mat

outer fabric: ½ yd. (0.5 m)

backing fabric: ½ yd. (0.5 m)

lining fabric: ½ yd. (0.5 m)

batting: 15" x 22" (38 x 56 cm), fusible by Hobbs

iron

sewing machine and walking foot or darning foot

thread

bath towel

clothes dryer

paint: Textile Color, Neopaque, or Lumiere by Jacquard

soft rubber brayer (available at craft and art supply stores)

pocket fabric: 5½" (14 cm) square (see step 4 for suggestions)

pins

ribbons: 1⅝ yd. (1.5 m) each of two different grosgrain ribbons for handles (one narrow, one wide)

embellishments for handle: yarn or trim, charms, beads (optional)

quilted/painted folder briefcase

Preparation
Cover your work surface with plastic.

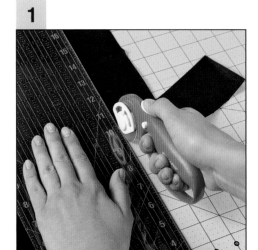

1 With a rotary cutter, ruler, and mat, measure and cut a piece of the outer fabric and a piece of backing 15" x 22" (38 x 56 cm) . Cut a lining piece 14" x 21" (35.5 x 53.5 cm).

2 Fuse the quilt sandwich together by using an iron to steam the backing to the batting and then steaming the outer fabric to the other side of the batting. Quilt all over the sandwich with a simple grid or other design, using a walking foot for machine-guided straight lines or a darning foot for free-motion curved lines. The pattern should be dense and consistent. Rinse the quilt sandwich in warm water to shrink the batting a little, blot in a towel, and dry in the dryer.

3

With the brayer, apply paint lightly over the surface of the quilt sandwich, covering the raised areas. You may want to practice with the brayer first to determine how much paint you want on it when you start printing. Allow the paint to dry. Heat set the paint with a dry iron. Trim the quilt sandwich to 14" x 21" (35.5 x 53.5 cm). Press the sandwich in half, wrong sides together, to create a guideline for handle and pocket placement.

4

Rubber stamp by Fred B. Mullett

The pocket can be a piece of artwork, a photo of your dog, another piece of quilting, or just a great chunk of fabric. To line the pocket, place it right sides together with a square of lining fabric and sew across the top and bottom edges with a ¼" (6 mm) seam. Turn the pocket right side out and press. Place it in the center of one side of the quilt sandwich and pin. Sew along the bottom edge.

Continued

5

Sew the narrow ribbon to the center of the wide ribbon. Starting at the fold, pin the sewn ribbon to the tote: cover ¼" (6 mm) of the sides of the pocket, extend to the top of the tote, allow 7" (18 cm) for a handle, start down the other side of the pocket, repeat the placement on the other side of the fold, and finish at the fold again. Turn under the raw edge of the ribbons and pin over the starting end. Sew down both sides of the ribbon, starting and ending 1" (2.5 cm) from the top edges. Embellish the handle with yarn, trim, charms, or beads, if desired.

6

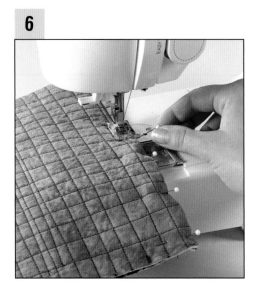

Sew the sides of the tote, right sides together, with a ¼" (6 mm) seam. Turn right side out.

7

Sew the lining in the same way, but leave a 3" or 4" (7.5 or 10 cm) opening in one side. Slip the outer tote into the lining, right sides together, and pin the raw edges, keeping the handles out of the way. Sew all around the top edge.

8

Pull the tote right side out through the opening in the lining seam. Sew the opening closed and press the tote and lining. Push the lining into the tote and topstitch around the upper edge, catching the handles for reinforcement. Buy some colored file folders to match your new tote!

Susan Suggests

Make your tote from a dark-colored quilt sandwich, and color it with this interesting technique. Working in a well-ventilated area, mix equal parts textile paint and discharge paste (both by Jacquard). Apply the mixture to the fabric (by brushing, rolling, or stamping), and allow it to dry. The discharge paste will remove the black color from the fabric and add the new color at the same time. Iron the quilt to reveal the new color.

sponge painting

Sponge painting is a quick and easy technique for creating textured patterns and backgrounds.

Small pieces of nonhardening sponge work well with medium-bodied fabric paints, and you can paint on wet or dry fabric to achieve different effects. Look for sponges that have holes of various sizes, and buy several so you always have a dry sponge ready for the next application. Use a transparent paint to fill in the background areas after the first sponge painting is dry.

materials and tools

Plastic cover for the table

Scissors

Freezer paper for palette and stencils

Iron

Stencil fabric: solid color

Acrylic stencils

Hydrophilic sponges:
yellow with rounded edges
(available at hobby stores or paint stores)

Metallic fabric paint: Lumiere

Background fabric

Medium-bodied, transparent fabric paint:
Textile Colors

Sea sponges
(available at wallpaper and paint stores)

Sheer fusible web: Misty-white Fuse

sponge painting

Sponging and stenciling combine for a textural treat.

Preparation
Protect your work surface with the plastic cover.

1

Cut a stencil out of freezer paper and iron the freezer paper to the stencil fabric. You can also use a pre-cut acrylic stencil. Cut the hydrophilic sponges into small, easy-to-hold pieces. Pour metallic paint onto a freezer-paper palette. Dip a sponge into the paint and then dab the sponge onto the freezer paper to remove the excess (don't go directly to the fabric or the sponge texture will not show on the first application).

2

Dab the paint on the fabric through the stencil openings. The less paint you have on the sponge, the more textured the design will look. Rinse the sponge and let the paint dry.

3

Create color movement and texture on the background fabric with another piece of sponge and the medium-bodied, transparent paint. Refill the sponge with paint as necessary. Devise your own pattern or follow the print on the fabric, if any. Use a variety of paint colors, if you wish. Try layering colors by dabbing a second color alongside of, and slightly overlapping, the first color. Allow the paint to dry.

4

Unify your color scheme by sponging transparent paint in a complementary color (see page 47) over the fabric using the sea sponge. Rinse your sponges in water to clean. Heat set the paint by ironing the fabric for three minutes or placing it in a hot dryer for 30 minutes.

Cut around the stenciled motif leaving a border of stencil fabric. This will ground the appliqué when it's fused to the background fabric. Attach the appliqué to the background fabric with fusible web.

Note: Stencil by Diane Ericson (see Resources).

Susan Suggests

If you like a watercolor look, spray the fabric with water either before or after painting with the fabric paint.

stamping with found objects

Rubber-stamping has been popular for years, but imagine other ways to stamp designs onto fabric.

Look around the house for common objects that could make unique prints. Check out your button box, desk, kitchen drawers, and workbench for items with interesting texture or items that can be carved or manipulated into patterns. A medium-bodied or a metallic paint works well for stamping because both retain the sharp edges you want. The key to making clear impressions with any stamping device is to load the stamp with enough paint to make a clear image, but not so much that the paint flows into the stamp's negative spaces. Work quickly when using fabric paint so it does not dry on the stamp.

materials and tools

Plastic cover for the table	Styrofoam trays
Glue for plastic: Goop	Ballpoint pen or toothpick
Buttons with flat contours and deep cuts	Sponge brush: 1" (2.5 cm)
Pill bottles or film canisters	Plexiglas and cardboard scraps
Spoon	Bubble wrap
Metallic fabric paint: Lumiere	String
Freezer paper or acrylic for a palette	Duct tape
Rubber brayer	Craft knife to carve erasers
Fabric	White erasers
Iron	Weather stripping

stamping with found objects

Fun stamping techniques
to use together or solo.

Preparation

Protect your work surface with the plastic cover. Before you begin, read through all of the techniques described in this section. One technique may contain a detailed instruction that is necessary for related techniques.

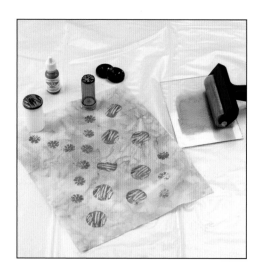

Button Stamping

Glue a button to the lid of an old pill bottle or film canister. Spoon paint onto your palette and smooth it out with the rubber brayer. Dip the button into the paint, then stamp the fabric. To keep the image distinct, load the stamp with paint each time you use it. For varied brightness, stamp two or three times before reloading with paint. Heat set the paint by ironing the fabric for three minutes or placing it in a hot dryer for 30 minutes.

Incised Styrofoam Stamping

Cut a rectangle from a Styrofoam tray. With a ballpoint pen or toothpick, draw several lines in the foam. Dab, don't brush, paint on the foam surface with a sponge brush (dabbing allows you to apply more paint). Turn the foam carved-side down on the fabric and rub the back of the foam to transfer the paint to the fabric. Do a test print before stamping your project because the foam will hold more paint the second time you use it. Heat set the paint when dry.

String and Bubble-Wrap Stamping

Wrap a Plexiglas or cardboard scrap with bubble wrap and another with string. Secure the bubble wrap in place on the back and form a handle with the duct tape. Spoon paint onto your palette and smooth it out with the rubber brayer. Dip the bubble wrap stamp into the paint, then stamp the fabric. Hold the string-wrapped stamp by one of the strings on the back and dip the front into the paint. Stamp the fabric. Heat set the paint when dry.

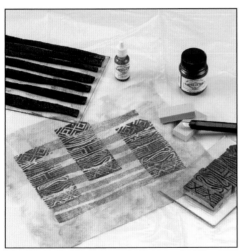

Carved-Eraser Stamping

Carve the erasers into your own one-of-a-kind designs and cut the weather stripping into shapes. Glue them separately or in a pattern to the Plexiglas scraps. Spoon paint onto your palette and smooth it out with the rubber brayer. Dip the stamps into the paint, then stamp the fabric. Heat set the paint when dry.

Note: Carved-eraser and weather-stripping stamps created by Diane Bartels.

Susan Suggests

Use an old toothbrush to clean out crevices if they clog while you're working.

nature printing

Flowers and leaves delight us during the growing season and are always nice to have around the rest of year.

Print and paint fabrics using natural materials, and you will enjoy the beauty of nature on wall hangings, quilts, household items, and clothing. Collect leaves and flowers any time of the year, press them between the pages of a thick phone book until they're dry, and then store them in plastic page protectors for future use. Simple flowers and leaves work best for printing and some will last through multiple uses.

materials and tools

Plastic cover for the table

Leaves

Phone book or other heavy book for pressing

Transparent fabric paint: Dye-na-Flow

Small spray bottle

Fabric

Newspaper

Sponge brushes: 1" (2.5 cm)

Opaque fabric paint: Neopaque, two or more colors

Rubber brayer

Metallic fabric paint: Lumiere

Iron

nature printing

Spray, brayer, accent—
three techniques to use alone
or to layer for autumnal bounty!

Preparation

Protect your work surface with the plastic cover. Press your leaves flat in a phone book or other heavy book for at least 20 minutes before use.

Spray

Pour the transparent paint into a small spray bottle. To produce a bold effect, use full-strength paint or for a softer look, dilute it with water. Place a large leaf on the fabric and spray the paint around the edges. Let the paint dry. Press with an iron to heat set when you complete your final Nature Printing technique.

Brayer: Preparation

Draw an outline the size of your journal page on the newspaper. Arrange the leaves inside the outline, vein-side (backside) up. Veining is more prominent on the back of leaves and offers a sharper image than you would get from the front. Remove the leaves one at a time from the newspaper, paint the backs with sponge brushes and two or more colors of opaque paint, and replace them in the design. Using variations of paint colors imitates the dappled hue of real leaves.

Brayer: Technique

Place a piece of fabric right side down over the leaves. Roll the brayer over it to transfer the paint to the fabric. Work quickly before the paint dries. This technique takes practice, so do several pieces and choose the best for your project. Peel the leaves off of the fabric and wipe them off if you want to use them again. Let the paint on the fabric dry for a few minutes.

Accent

To add an accent, spread metallic paint on another leaf, place it paint side down in the design, and brayer over it to transfer the paint to the fabric. Heat set the fabric with an iron when completely dry.

Susan Suggests

After your images are printed, dried, and heat set, they can be outlined with a permanent black marker or highlighted with stitching.

monoprinting

Monoprinting is a tried and true printing method that produces one-of-a-kind freeform designs.

The process involves manipulating paints on a nonporous surface such as marble, glass, or hard plastic, then pressing fabric onto the paint and lifting to create the unique artwork.

You can make a wonderful print on two pieces of fabric and keep everything contained in a plastic sheet protector while you are working! It's like finger painting without touching the paint!

A metallic paint works beautifully for this method, and the prints can be done on black fabric for dramatic results. The finished prints will be mirror images of each other. The possibilities for vest fronts, coordinated purse panels, or interesting wall hangings are unlimited.

materials and tools

Plastic cover for the table

Plastic sheet protector
(available at office supply stores)

Metallic fabric paint:
Lumiere, two or three colors

Spoons or wooden craft sticks to use with the paint

Fabric: black, approximately 9" x 12"
(22.9 x 30.5 cm)

monoprinting

A fun process that creates its own statement.

Preparation

Protect your work surface with the plastic cover.

1

Cut two edges off the sheet protector, leaving one connected edge. Open the sheet protector on the plastic-covered table. Shake or stir the paint thoroughly and spoon the paint onto one side of the plastic. Use two or three colors that coordinate with or complement each other.

2

Close the sheet protector. Manipulate the paint by pushing with your fingers so paint covers most of the area inside the plastic. Work quickly so the paint does not bead up or start to dry. Open the sheet protector.

3

Place one piece of fabric on each side of the sheet protector, then close it. Quickly and *gently* rub both sides of the plastic to transfer the paint to the fabric. Do not push the paint into the grain of the fabric or the colors will appear dull.

4

Remove the fabric pieces from the sheet protector and separate them. Let them dry flat on the plastic-covered table for 24 hours. Heat set the paint with an iron set to the proper temperature for the fabric for 30 seconds on both sides of the fabric, or place the fabric in a hot dryer for 30 minutes.

Susan Suggests

You can use an 18" x 12" (45.7 x 30.5 cm) folded piece of fabric for a butterfly effect. Be very careful when placing the fabric within the sheet protector.

monoprinted placemats

Monoprinting is a very old method for printing on paper, using ink and a marble slab.

Today we can print our own fabric using textile paint and a piece of plastic or glass. First you apply paint to the surface and manipulate it. You can use many methods for drawing in the paint—all fun and rather playful. Then you lay the fabric over the paint and roll over it to transfer the design. Often you can get a second print from the paint that is left over, and sometimes it's better than the first! When the paint is dry, heat set it with an iron, and make some great new placemats for your table.

materials and tools

plastic cover for the table

center fabric: ½ yd. (0.5 m)

border/backing fabric: 1⅓ yd. (1.2 m)

batting: cotton/polyester, crib size

iron

rotary cutter, acrylic ruler, and mat

masking tape

piece of template plastic or glass with taped edges: at least 10" x 14" (25.5 x 35.5 cm)

permanent black marker

paint: Lumiere by Jacquard

sponge brushes: 1" (2.5 cm)

rubber or foam stamp

paper towels

soft rubber brayer (available at craft and art supply stores)

spray bottle filled with water

one 12" x 16" (30.5 x 40.5 cm) piece of mat board or heavy cardboard

pins

sewing machine

thread

monoprinted placemats

Preparation
Cover your work surface with plastic.

1

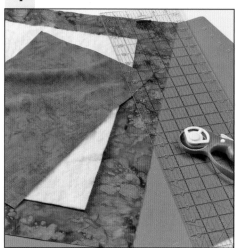

Preshrink the fabrics and batting. Iron the fabric smooth. With a rotary cutter, ruler, and mat, measure and cut four 9" x 13" (23 x 33 cm) pieces of the center fabric. Cut four 17" x 21" (43 x 53 cm) pieces of the border/backing fabric. Cut four 12" x 16" (30.5 x 40.5 cm) pieces of batting.

2

Tape the plastic or glass to the table to make it easier to pull the fabric off the paint. Draw a 9" x 13" (23 x 33 cm) rectangle on the plastic with a marker. Apply the Lumiere paint to the plastic within the drawn rectangle with a sponge brush. Try to apply enough paint to minimize brush marks but not so much that the paint will spread out everywhere when you print the fabric. But, as always, imperfections show the mark of the artist and are what make your work unique! Work quickly so the paint does not dry on the plastic.

3

With the stamp, pick up paint from the plastic by pressing down hard and lifting straight up. Wipe the stamp on paper towel between each use. Randomly stamp until there is pattern all over the painted area. Work quickly so the paint does not dry.

4

Lay the center fabric facedown on top of the paint, being careful not to smear the design. Roll the brayer over the top of the fabric so the paint transfers to the fabric. Pull the fabric straight up off the plastic and set aside to dry. Repeat the process for three more pieces of fabric. Heat set the paint by ironing the fabric on the back with a dry iron for 30 seconds on each area.

Continued

Print Variation

To make two prints from one paint setup, spray water onto the paint that remains on the plastic after printing the first piece of fabric. Lay a second piece of fabric over it. Roll the brayer over the fabric to transfer the paint. The second print will be much lighter and show the pattern of the spray.

5

Press under the edges of the border/backing fabric ½" (1.3 cm) all the way around. Center the mat board on the wrong side of the border/backing, and press the edges up and over the board. To miter the corners, first fold in the corner diagonally and press. Then fold in the sides to meet in the center of the corner. After pressing, remove the mat board.

6

Place the batting piece in the center of the border/backing aligning it to the outer the folds. Center the printed piece over the batting, tucking the edges under the folded edges of the border. Pin.

7

Topstitch the edges of the border through all the layers. Quilt the center around the printed motifs if you wish.

Susan Suggests

Use the monoprinting technique to make a table runner. Follow the same steps, adjusting the measurements to suit your project. Make napkins with satin-stitched or serged edges to match.

splash and puddle painting

Dye-na-Flow paint, a very thin paint that acts like a dye, flows over the surface of and mixes readily on fabric.

One of the advantages of using paint instead of dye is immediately seeing your colors blend and patterns develop. You'll have *no* control over what the paints do after you apply them to the fabric, which generates extra fun!

You'll quickly grasp color theory as you watch primary colors (red, yellow, blue) mix together to form secondary colors (purple, green, orange) and see complementary colors (see page 47) blend to make earth tones.

In this sample, the complementary colors purple and yellow formed brown when they bled into each other.

Try a piece of silk or pima cotton for this project, as these fabrics are easy to manipulate.

materials and tools

Plastic cover for the table

Fabric: China silk or silk twill (8 to 12 mm) or pima cotton

Transparent fabric paint: Dye-na-Flow, assorted colors

Pipettes or eyedroppers

Spray bottle containing water

Sponge brushes: 1" (2.5 cm)

Coarse salt

Iron

Bubble wrap

Heavy-duty aluminum foil

Masking tape

Note: Prepared for dyeing (PFD) fabric works best.

splash and puddle painting

Once you try the various techniques separately, **mix and match them** for spontaneous, interesting patterns.

Preparation

Protect your work surface with the plastic cover. Before you begin, read through all of the techniques described in this section. One technique may contain a detailed instruction that is necessary for related techniques.

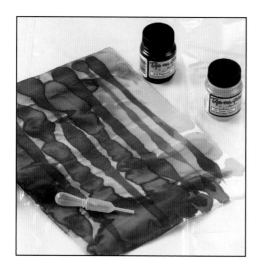

Create a Background

Lay a piece of fabric on your work surface. You will create this pattern using one or more colors, as desired. Dribble paint with a pipette or eyedropper across the fabric in parallel lines. Now dribble paint onto the fabric in lines that are perpendicular to the first lines. Leave some white space for the paint to flow into. After a couple of minutes, add more paint if you think there is too much white space, or spray the fabric with water to make the paint run.

Salt Patterning

Spray the fabric with water. Paint a random pattern over the entire surface with two or three colors, using a separate sponge brush for each color. Spray the fabric with more water to make the colors blend. Immediately sprinkle coarse salt over the surface. Let the fabric dry slowly to allow the salt to push the paint into fascinating configurations. Wrinkles in the plastic or ripples in the fabric will also form designs. After the fabric dries, brush off the salt, heat set the fabric with the iron or in a dryer for 30 minutes, then wash out any salt residue.

Bubble-Wrap Patterning

Lay a piece of bubble wrap on the table, bubble side up. Lay a piece of fabric over it and spray the fabric with water. Paint a random pattern over the entire surface of the fabric with one or more colors, using a separate sponge brush for each color. As you work, push the brush down into the valleys created by the bubble wrap. Spray the fabric with more water until you see distinct circle patterns. Allow the fabric to dry completely, then press to heat set the paint.

Color Pleating

Cut a piece of heavy-duty aluminum foil to the size of your fabric (a fat quarter, 18" x 22" [45.7 x 55.9 cm], or a smaller piece works well). Use masking tape to attach the ends of the fabric to the foil. Crease the foil and fabric together into 1" (2.5 cm) pleats. Unfold the pleats slightly. Place the pleated fabric and foil on your table. Spray the fabric with water. Using enough paint so the colors will be able to blend together on the sides of the mountains and in the valleys, apply a color with a sponge brush on the mountains. Using a separate sponge brush, apply another color in the valleys. After the paint dries, press the fabric flat, using a heat setting appropriate to the fabric, to reveal a wonderful soft stripe and to set the paint.

Susan Suggests

The color wheel can help guide you through color choices. Complementary colors are yellow/purple, blue/orange, and red/green. Here is an easy way to remember this: the complement of any primary color is the combination of the other two primary colors.

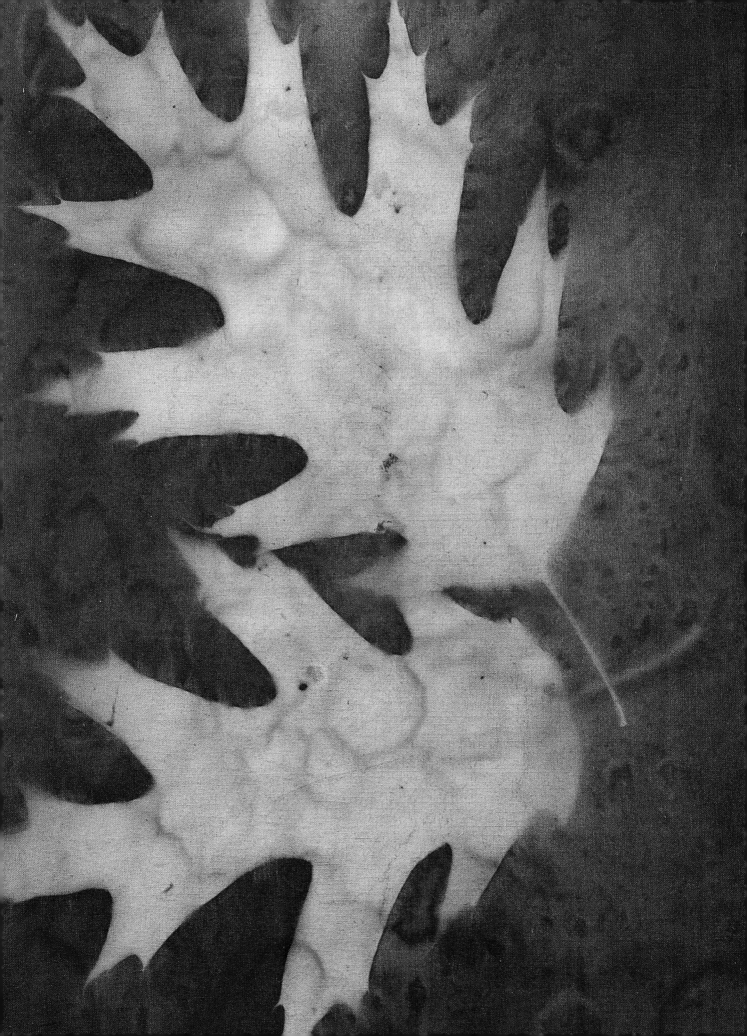

sunprinting with paint

Sunprinting is an exciting and delightfully simple technique that uses the sun to imprint images on cloth.

The entire surface of a fabric is painted, objects are arranged on it, and the fabric is dried in direct sunlight. The color under the objects lightens, but the brilliant color of the painted fabric exposed to the sun remains.

The intensity of the sun affects the quality of the prints, so plan ahead and have your materials ready for when the weather cooperates. Make sun blocks from items found around the house and yard. Each will make a distinct pattern. If the day is breezy, weigh down your objects with small stones or tape netting over them. Do not use glass or another solid cover because it will prevent the paint from drying and printing your image.

materials and tools

Plastic cover for the table

Fabric: light-colored, flat, and wrinkle-free

Foam core or plywood: plastic-covered

Spray bottle containing water

Transparent fabric paint: Dye-na-Flow

Sponge brush: 1" (2.5 cm)

Sun blocks: leaves, rice, macaroni, torn cheesecloth, or plastic letters

Small stones, glass marbles, or netting (optional)

Iron

sunprinting with paint

A quick and easy process **that creates looks from** sophisticated to whimsical.

Preparation
Protect your work surface with the plastic cover.

1

Place the fabric on a plastic-covered board. Any threads lying on the surface of the fabric or the board will create a print and so will folds or wrinkles in the plastic. Spray the fabric with water until damp.

2

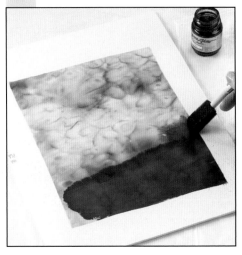

Paint the entire surface of the damp fabric with paint using a sponge brush. Take the paint straight out of the bottle. Work quickly so the paint stays wet, as dry paint will not print.

3

Place your sun blocks on top of the fabric. Spray the fabric with water again and press the edges of the objects firmly into the wet paint. They must lie flat; edges that are not flat against the fabric allow sun underneath and you will not get a clear, sharp print. Weigh down the objects, if necessary, with small stones or glass marbles, or tape a piece of netting over the project if the weather is breezy. The netting will print, but that adds an interesting secondary design. Place the project in direct sunlight.

4

When the fabric has dried completely, remove the objects. Heat set the paint by ironing the fabric for three minutes or placing it in a hot dryer for 30 minutes. Be sure to look at the back of the fabric—sometimes it is as pretty as the front!

Susan Suggests

Try layering your sunprints. After printing and drying your fabric, repaint with another color and use the same or different objects to print the fabric for a luscious layered effect.

resisting paint

You can control where paint flows over fabric or where it remains after it's applied.

Numerous intriguing methods, some mechanical and some chemical block paint from certain areas of the fabric. Each is called a "resist." Mechanical resists range from the fine hand-stitching of Japanese shibori to clothespins clamped on folds in the fabric. Chemical resists like gutta allow you to paint lovely florals or other images with precision. Potato dextrin dries on a fabric and forms a network of fine cracks that allows paint or dye to seep into them. For this project, simple school glue was used as a chemical resist and then washed out.

Try the methods shown here for quick, dramatic results. Different paint viscosities (consistencies) provide different results, so play with several to see what works best. As always, heat set the paint after it dries to make it permanent.

materials and tools

Plastic cover for the table	Container of warm water to dissolve glue
Fabric: white, preferably PFD	Toothbrush
Glue: Elmer's Washable School Glue Gel (the blue kind)	Masking tape, stickers, or adhesive shelf paper
Medium-bodied fabric paint: Textile Colors	String
Sponge brushes: 1" (2.5 cm)	Transparent fabric paint: Dye-na-Flow
Spray bottle containing water	Scissors
Iron	Rubber bands

painted tabletop screen

A small accordion-folded screen, displayed on a table or bookshelf, is a pretty way to show off your favorite painting techniques.

This screen was designed using different types of Jacquard paints. The techniques include resist painting, painting a plaid, sun printing, salt patterning, bubble wrap printing, and painting over pleated foil. Add quotations or poetry with Mistyfuse web and ExtravOrganza inkjet fabric sheets, if you like.

materials and tools

plastic cover for the table

fabric: 9" x 11" (23 x 28 cm), white and colored

masking tape

paint: Lumiere and Dye-na-Flow by Jacquard

sponge brushes: 1" (2.5 cm)

masking objects: leaves, paper cutouts, rice, pasta

coarse salt

bubble wrap

scissors

heavy-duty aluminum foil: 9" x 11" (23 x 28 cm)

spray bottle of water

iron

fusible web: Wonder-Under

heavy interfacing: five 9" x 11" (23 x 28 cm) pieces, Peltex or Timtex

rotary cutter, acrylic ruler, and mat

backing and "hinge" fabric: 1¼ yd. (1.15 m)

sewing machine

thread

painted tabletop screen

Preparation
Cover your work surface with plastic.

Resist-Painted Stripes

Choose a colored piece of fabric for this technique. You may want to do two pieces and choose the one you like best for the finished project. Cut pieces of masking tape the length of the fabric and tear the pieces into two long strips with irregular widths. Press the tape onto the fabric. Using Lumiere paint, brush paint between the tape strips until the exposed fabric is covered. Remove the tape and let the fabric dry.

Painted Plaid

On dampened white fabric, paint two colors of Dye-na-Flow in parallel lines. While the first colors are still wet, paint a third color across the first lines to blend the colors, leaving some white space for the paint to bleed into. Let dry.

Sun Print

Cover a dampened, colored fabric piece (7" [18 cm] square) with dark colored Dye-na-Flow paint. Place a leaf, paper cutout, rice or pasta, coarse lace, or other mask on top of the painted fabric and press down so the edges are tight to the surface. Put out in direct sun and let dry. When the fabric is dry, the mask shapes should be the color of the original fabric and the background should be dark. Trim the square to 5" or 6" (12.5 or 15 cm).

Salt Patterning

Paint the entire surface of dampened white fabric with Dye-na-Flow. It should be quite wet. Throw coarse salt onto the wet paint and allow it to dry without disturbing it. The salt will pull the paint into interesting patterns.

Continued

Bubble Wrap Print

With the sponge brush and one or two colors of Lumiere paint, brush paint onto the raised side of bubble wrap. Place colored fabric facedown over the bubble wrap and press the back with your hand. Remove the fabric and let dry.

Paint Over Pleated Foil

Cut a piece of heavy-duty aluminum foil the same size as a piece of white fabric. Spray the fabric to dampen it. Fold the foil and fabric together into 1" (2.5 cm) accordion pleats. Pull out the pleats so you have peaks and valleys, and set it on the plastic-covered table. Paint one color of Dye-na-Flow paint on the peaks and another color in the valleys until the colors start to blend. Spray with more water if you want to encourage more blending. Allow to dry on the foil.

1

Heat set all of the fabric pieces by ironing them from the back for 30 seconds on all areas. Fuse the painted pieces to the interfacing with Wonder-Under, following the manufacturer's directions. With a rotary cutter, ruler, and mat, measure and cut five pieces of backing fabric the same size and fuse to the back of the interfacing pieces. Trim the "pages" down to 8" x 10" (20.5 x 25.5 cm). Fuse the sun print to one of the painted pieces. Stitch around the edges of the sun print and all of the pages using a close zigzag stitch.

2

Cut a 19" x 42" (48.5 x 106.5 cm) piece of hinge fabric. Fold the hinge right sides together lengthwise and sew around the raw edges with a ¼" (6 mm) seam, leaving a 3" (7.5 cm) opening. Trim the corners and turn right side out through the opening; press. Lay the "pages" on the hinge so the ends match and there is a tiny space between the pages. Sew down each side of the pages through all the layers.

Susan Suggests

When you design small pieces such as the ones in this project, make extras and put them in a plastic bin marked "Miscellaneous." Then when you start a new project or collage, you will have assorted items already prepared. Even things you don't like can be used as backgrounds for stamping, needle felting, or layering.

lasagna dyeing

This method, also called "painting silk layers," makes it fun and exciting to paint several pieces of silk at the same time.

You'll stack four or five layers of silk pieces and then paint the surface with a free-flowing textile paint. This very thin paint gives the effect of dyeing without the mess and chemicals. The paint sinks through the fabric layers and creates a variety of patterns, depending on the absorbency and the position of the fabric in the stack. The colors blend together and always produce a surprise.

I painted my project pieces with magenta and turquoise and then applied golden yellow. Suddenly, orange, bright green, and yellow sprang to life.

Wait for all the layers to dry (the hardest part of all!), then peel them apart to reveal the wonderful results.

materials and tools

Plastic cover for the table

Silk in four or five weaves

Iron

Nozzle-tipped squeeze bottles, pipettes, or eyedroppers

Transparent fabric paint: Dye-na-Flow in magenta, turquoise, and golden yellow

White cotton fabric for the backing

Sheer fusible web: Misty-white Fuse

Cooking parchment (available at grocery stores)

Ribbon to cover edges

lasagna dyeing

Work step-by-step into a surprise ending.

Preparation
Protect your work surface with the plastic cover.

1

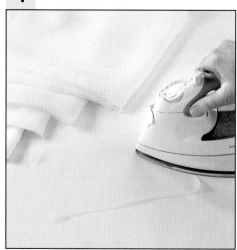

Cut four or five pieces of silk to the same size—6" to 9" (15.2 to 22.9 cm) squares work well. Set the iron to the temperature for silk and press to remove all wrinkles. Stack the pieces together. Do not pin them because the pin would attract the paint, and a little shifting is fine.

2

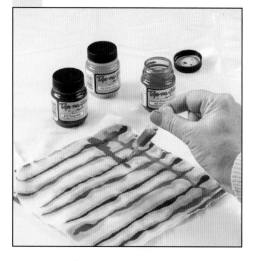

Fill two or three nozzle-tipped squeeze bottles, pipettes, or eyedroppers with separate colors of transparent paint, and create lines or patterns on the top layer of silk. Leave some white space as you work. The paint will flow freely as it dries, generating its own design.

Note: Avoid using colors opposite each other on the color wheel (red/green, blue/orange, purple/yellow) because they make muddy colors when mixed.

3

Peel the silk layers apart when they are dry. Notice how the pattern differs greatly depending on the weave of the silk and the position of the fabric in the stack. Press the pieces to set the paint.

4

Cut a piece of cotton fabric the size you want for your finished project. Cover it with a layer of fusible web. Arrange the silk pieces into a pleasing composition, cover it with a piece of cooking parchment, and fuse. Sew or fuse the ribbon over the edges.

Susan Suggests

For the various silk weaves, choose netting, crinkle chiffon, patterned organza, and habotai. Look for silk fabrics with woven-in designs for extra impact.

lasagna painted silk throw

There is nothing that feels as lovely as silk, but did you know it can be less expensive than cotton?!

Look for China silk, silk twill, crinkle chiffon, silk with motifs woven into it, organza, and other silks that have similar weights. Pile up squares of the different pieces and pour on Dye-na-Flow paint. Walk away for a few hours, and then peel apart the layers to reveal gorgeous colors and patterns. Back the squares with batting and a print fabric, quilt along the printed motifs, and you have the makings of the most luxurious throw you've ever seen!

materials and tools

plastic cover for the table

silk fabrics: twelve 22" (56 cm) squares of various natural-colored silks, all of similar weights (8 to 12 mummie)

plastic pipettes or eyedroppers

paints: Dye-na-Flow by Jacquard (I used golden yellow, azure blue, and brilliant red)

iron

clothes dryer

batting: Hobbs queen-size fusible

rotary cutter, acrylic ruler, and mat

cotton fabrics: six ⅝ yd. (0.6 m) pieces of coordinated cotton fabrics for backing (should have large patterns that can be quilted around)

sewing machine

darning foot

thread

quilting gloves (optional)

scissors

ribbon: 10 yd. (9.15 m) to match painted silk, 1" (2.5 cm) wide and straight-of-grain

binding fabric: ½ yd. (0.5 m)

lasagna painted silk throw

Preparation

Cover your work surface with plastic. If you are unfamiliar with this technique, experiment on a small stack of silk fabrics before you begin your project.

1

Collect silks of several different weaves and patterns, keeping in mind that you want it to have a little body (about the weight of a typical silk scarf) so it will be easy to handle. Cut or tear twelve 22" (56 cm) squares of fabric. You will be cutting down the size slightly after the quilting is completed. Press all creases out of the silk because the paint will follow them. Divide the silk pieces into three stacks of four pieces each. Do not pin them.

2

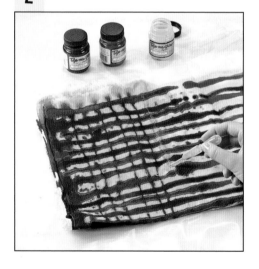

Using a separate pipette or eyedropper for each color, dribble paint onto the top piece of each stack. Create a grid or other pattern that covers much of the fabric but leaves some white space, since the paint will flow for some time after you apply it. The bottom layers will collect a lot of paint, so too much paint will make the colors muddy, but not enough paint will leave too much white on the top layer. Work quickly so the colors blend. For variety, use a different order or pattern on each stack. Note that different silks have different absorbency rates, regardless of their thickness.

3

After the paint is completely dry, carefully pull the layers apart. Heat set the paint by ironing each piece for 3 minutes, or throw the pieces in the clothes dryer on high for 30 minutes.

4

Place the fusible batting in the dryer for 5 minutes on delicate to remove the wrinkles and preshrink it. Preshrink the backing fabrics by ironing them with steam. Use a rotary cutter, ruler, and mat to cut the backing fabrics into twelve 22" (56 cm) squares and fuse them to the batting using lots of steam. The other side of the batting will stick to your ironing surface, but it peels off readily. Trim the batting to fit.

Continued

5

Steam-iron the silk pieces to the other side of the batting sandwiches. Sizes may not match exactly, but the squares will be trimmed after the quilting is completed.

6

Drop the feed dogs on your machine and put on the darning foot. Quilt around the motifs on the backing fabrics (you don't have to follow the lines on the print exactly). Remember that the bobbin thread will be what shows on the silk side of your quilt sandwiches. Make sure the density of the quilting remains fairly consistent from one sandwich to the other. Wearing quilting gloves helps you move the sandwiches more easily.

7

After quilting, cut the sandwiches down to 20½" (52 cm) square. Arrange the pieces in four rows of three sandwiches, balancing the colors and patterns. Sew the pieces of each row together with ¼" (6 mm) seams, stitching through all the layers. Sew the seams with the backing sides together so the seam allowances show on the silk side. Press the seam allowances open, as flat as possible. Sew the rows together, matching seam intersections.

8

Center the ribbon over the seams on the silk side, covering the seam allowances. Sew close to both edges. The back of the quilt will have sewn lines parallel to the seams. After all the seam allowances are covered, bind the quilt.

A quick and easy variation: Buy a pre-hemmed silk scarf blank, 12" x 60" (30.5 x 152 cm), and fold it into five 12" (30.5 cm) sections. Paint the top layer, let it stand until dry, unfold, and heat set. A designer scarf for under $5!

Susan Suggests

If you can't find ribbon to match your painted silks, buy white ribbon and paint it with the same colors as your fabrics. Remember that paint, unlike dye, can be used on any fiber content, so you can use polyester or rayon ribbon if you like. Remember to heat set it just like the fabric, using a temperature appropriate for the fiber.

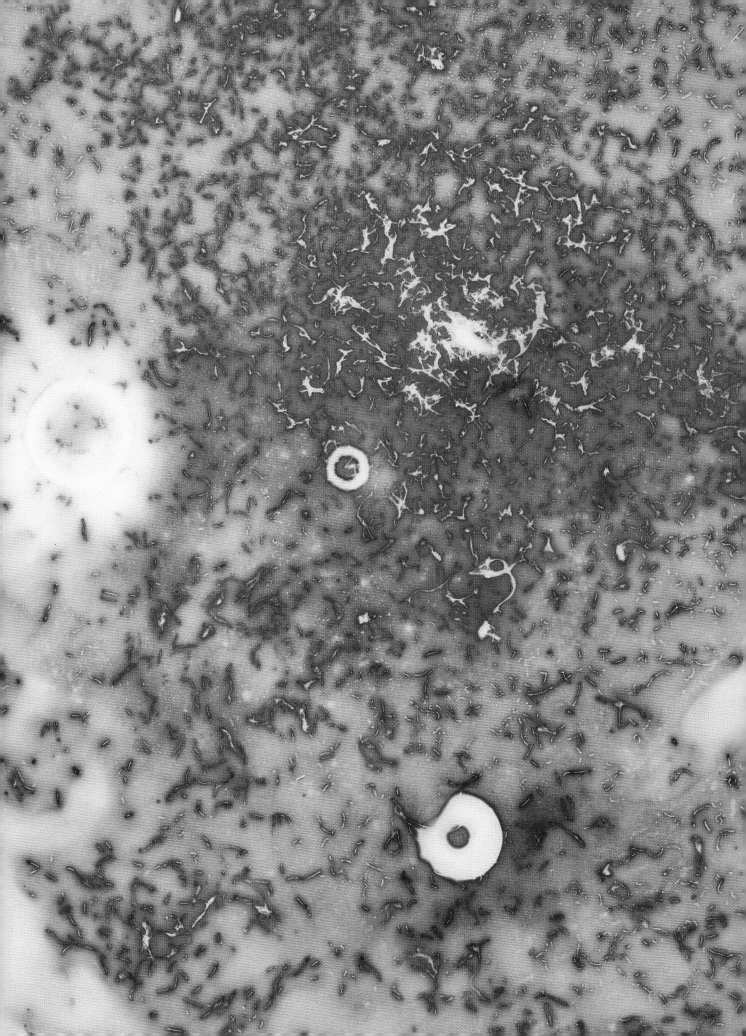

rust dyeing

You may have produced rust-dyed fabric by mistake.

Now fiber artists are making rust art by design! Using metal pans, steel wool, hardware, old grates, and rusty metal found in the street you can create lovely patterns on white or colored silk or cotton fabric. This is another technique where you can expect the unexpected to create something truly unique. Start combing the house and street for old metal!

materials and tools

Plastic cover for the table

White PFD cotton, hand-dyed fabric, or silk scarves

Tray to hold fabric (a rusty one works great)

Spray bottle

Water

White vinegar

Rubber gloves

Flat metal objects such as washers, not galvanized

Steel wool

Drawstring garbage bag large enough to fit around the tray

Heavy objects to use for pressing (optional)

Container with ¼ cup (60 ml) salt dissolved in 4 gallons (16 l) of hot water

Soap

rust dyeing

You will never look at junk metal the same way after trying this process.

Preparation
Protect your work surface with the plastic cover.

1

Lay the fabric on the tray. Spray it with a solution of approximately half vinegar and half water.

2

Put on rubber gloves and lay metal objects and shredded steel wool on the wet fabric. Use special care when handling metal that is already rusty. Spray again with vinegar-water.

3

Place the tray inside the garbage bag and tie up the opening. The fabric needs to stay wet for twenty-four hours in order for the metal to rust and color the fabric. I weighted down the top of the bag with books to press the steel wool to the fabric.

4

Put on rubber gloves. Remove the bag and then remove the metal pieces and steel wool from the fabric and store them for further use. Neutralize the rust by soaking the fabric in the salt-water solution. Wash the fabric in soapy water.

Susan Suggests

Be sure to use one of the fabric types listed in the materials list. They have no finishes on them that would prevent the rust from coloring the fabric.

rust-dyed silk scarf

Beauty can come from humble beginnings. Although rust stains are something we usually avoid, this project promotes them!

The wonderfully rich-colored surface of this silk scarf was created by staining it with rust. After being trapped inside a plastic bag with wet metal findings and steel wool fibers, a once plain scarf emerged as a truly unique work of art. Soon you will be searching nooks and crannies and even the street for castoff metal pieces with interesting shapes.

materials and tools

plastic cover for the table

nongalvanized metal objects: washers, gears, architectural elements

plastic or metal tray

rubber gloves

nongalvanized steel wool

hemmed silk scarf: 9" x 54" (23 x 137 cm) or size of your choice

spray bottle

vinegar

garbage bag

heavy books

basin

measuring cup

salt

wire cutters

stovepipe wire

sandpaper

PVC pipe, about 12" (30.5 cm) long

rust-dyed silk scarf

Preparation
Cover your work surface with plastic.

1

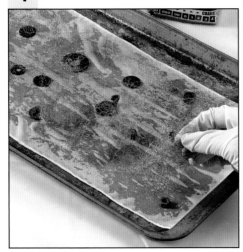

Place some of the metal objects in the tray. Put on the rubber gloves to protect your hands and shred some steel wool over the bottom. Fold the scarf to fit into the tray over the metal objects. Spray the scarf with a solution of half vinegar, half water. It should be quite wet.

2

Lay more metal objects on the top layer of the scarf. Shred more of the steel wool, sprinkling it over the entire surface. Spray the metal with the vinegar-water solution.

3

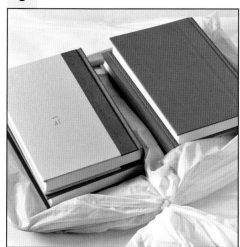

Place the tray in a garbage bag and close the end. Weight the metal objects down with heavy books so they maintain good contact with the scarf. Place the tray in a warm place for 24 hours or until you like the amount of rusting (sometimes as little as 2 hours makes a nice design).

4

Wearing the gloves, remove the tray from the plastic bag and take off all of the metal objects and steel wool. In a basin, mix ¼ cup (60 ml) of salt in 4 gallons (16 l) of hot water. Soak the scarf to neutralize the rust. Wash the scarf in soapy water, rinse, and dry.

Continued

1

Rust and Wrinkles

For another look, lay the scarf out flat on a plastic-covered table. Spray it with vinegar-water. Cover the surface with shredded steel wool.

2

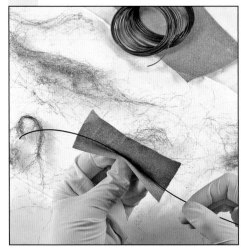

Cut a piece of stovepipe wire several inches longer than the length of the scarf. Fold a piece of sand-paper in half and run the wire through it to remove the protective coating. Lay the wire down the length of the scarf.

3

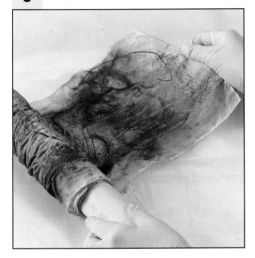

Roll the scarf onto a PVC pipe, curving the wire as you go. Wrap any remaining wire around the scarf to hold it on the pipe. Scrunch the scarf together sideways to create wrinkles. Spray with vinegar-water again. Place in a garbage bag for 24 hours or until the rusting is complete. Unwrap the scarf from the pipe, neutralize, wash, and dry.

Rusted Cotton Scarf

Scrunch hand-dyed cotton fabrics and layer them in a plastic zipper bag with steel wool and vinegar-water. Allow the fabric to rust. Wash and dry the fabric. Cut it into 3½" (7.5 cm) squares. Sew them together in 24 rows of three squares, and topstitch the outer edge. Wash or brush the seam allowances to fray them, for a casual look.

Susan Suggests

If you use rust-dyed fabric for piecing or appliqué, be aware that the fabric will be harder to stitch through. Use a microtex/sharp needle.

screen printing

Screen printing is a great way to quickly apply repeated images to fabric.

You can cover a large piece of fabric for a garment or print lots of the same image on small cuts of fabric. You can make screen prints in several different ways, but some methods, such as thermography and photo emulsion, are more complex than others. Here, with simple stretcher bars and polyester mesh from the art supply store, you'll discover how to make your own screen and create images with sticky-back plastic.

materials and tools

Plastic cover for the table

Hammer

Stretcher bars: two 10" or 11"
(25.4 or 27. 9 cm) and two 12" (30.5 cm)

Scissors

Polyester mesh: 10xx – 14xx weave

Stapler

Duct tape

Toothbrush to clean mesh

Scouring powder to clean mesh

Sticky-back drawer-lining plastic

Craft knife

Newspaper

Fabric

Opaque fabric paint:
Neopaque, assorted colors

Squeegee

Bristle brush: small artist's

Iron

screen printing

With a small assembly of wood and mesh, a few **cuts in sticky-back plastic, and a handy** squeegee, create your personal style statement in cloth.

Preparation
Protect your work surface with the plastic cover.

1

Pound the stretcher bars together until the frame is tight. Cut a piece of polyester mesh to approximately the outside measurements of the frame and staple it to the wood, stretching the mesh as taut as you can. Cover all the wood frame around the mesh with duct tape, extending the tape onto the exposed mesh about ½" (1.3 cm); repeat the taping on the back of the frame. Scrub the mesh with the toothbrush and scouring powder to open all the holes in the weave completely.

2

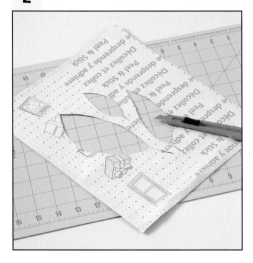

Cut a piece of sticky-back plastic slightly smaller than the outside measurements of the frame. Cut a design in the center using the craft knife. Keep the area of the design about ½" (1.3 cm) smaller than the exposed mesh on all edges. Remove the protective paper from the plastic, adhere it to the front of the mesh (the side that will be flush against the fabric), and rub it onto the mesh firmly.

3

Put a thick pad of newspaper on the table and lay a piece of fabric on it, right side up. Place the frame on top of the fabric, with the design touching the fabric. Pour about 2 tablespoons (30 ml) of the paint onto the tape along one edge of the frame. The exact amount of paint you need will depend on the openness of your design. You can use two or three colors if you like. Apply firm pressure and pull the paint across the mesh with the squeegee. You may need to do two or three passes. It takes practice to know how much pressure to use, since too much will force paint underneath the edges of the design opening.

4

To avoid smearing the paint as you lift the frame, hold the fabric down with one hand and carefully pull the frame straight up. Touch up any leaks or missed spots with the brush. Continue to print images so you have a selection to choose from (you will likely have some rejects at the beginning). Let the paint dry. Scrub the screen immediately so the paint does not clog the mesh. Heat set the paint with an iron after it is completely dry.

Susan Suggests

Use a thick viscosity paint to keep the color from seeping under the edges of your design. If you do not have a squeegee, try using an old credit card.

screen-printed pillowcase

What child wouldn't love to have a personal pillowcase? Make one from fun fabric and screen print the child's name on the hem band.

Or make some artful pillowcases for your own bed, possibly matched to the quilt or a painting in the room. Although some techniques for making the screens are more high-tech, this method of screen printing is easy to do and the materials are readily available.

materials and tools

plastic cover for the table

pillowcase fabric: 7/8 yd. (0.8 m) cotton

accent fabric: 1/3 yd. (0.32 m)

iron

rotary cutter, acrylic ruler, and mat

printing screen, approximately 10" x 12" (25.5 x 30.5 cm) (available at art supply stores)

duct tape

cleanser and toothbrush

sticky-back plastic shelf liner: 10" x 12" (25.5 x 30.5 cm)

commercial letter stencils (optional)

craft knife

newspaper

paint: Neopaque by Jacquard

credit card or screen-printing squeegee

old towel

small paintbrush

sewing machine

thread

screen-printed pillowcase

Preparation
Cover your work surface with plastic.

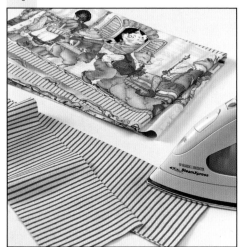

Preshrink the fabrics and iron them smooth. Using a rotary cutter, ruler, and mat, measure and cut the main fabric to 27" x 40" (68.5 x 101.5 cm). Cut the hem band 9" x 40" (23 x 101.5 cm). Press the hem band in half in both directions, wrong sides together, to mark the position for printing.

Cover all the wood of the printing screen frame with duct tape, extending the tape onto the exposed mesh about ½" (1.3 cm); repeat the taping on the other side of the frame. Scrub the mesh with cleanser and a toothbrush to open all the holes in the weave completely. Rinse and dry thoroughly.

3

Draw your design or stencil your lettering on the protective paper side of the shelf liner. Make sure your design will fit into a 3½" x 8" (9 x 20.5 cm) space. Use the craft knife to cut out the design. If you want to include a name plus another motif in a different color, cut two stencils and use two screens.

4

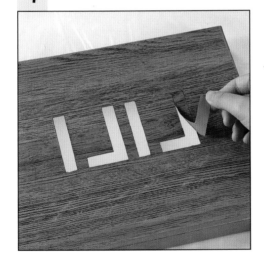

Pull off the protective paper from the shelf liner and press the sticky side to the back of the screen (the side that will lie flat on the fabric). Your lettering should read correctly when the screen is laid on the fabric.

Continued

screen-printed pillowcase (continued)

5

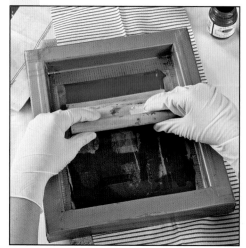

Place a pad of newspaper on your plastic-covered table. Turn the screen so the stencil is flat against the paper. Pour one or two colors of paint onto one end of the screen and squeegee it across the screen so the design in the stencil is printed clearly onto the paper. It might take a little practice to determine how much pressure is needed: too little will not put enough paint on the paper and too much will push paint under the openings in the stencil.

Place the hem band on an old towel, making sure the design is centered on the correct quarter section of the hem band, and screen print the design onto the fabric.

6

Carefully pull the screen straight up and off of the fabric. Touch up any missed spots with a small paintbrush. If you are only making the one print, remove the shelf liner from the screen immediately and wash the screen with a brush to remove all traces of paint. Let the painted fabric dry thoroughly. If you are using two screens, add the additional motifs, let dry again, and then iron the fabric for 30 seconds with a hot iron to set the paint.

7

Sew the hem band to the main fabric, with the right side of the hem band against the wrong side of the main fabric. Sew with a ½" (1.3 cm) seam allowance. Press the seam toward the hem band. Press under ½" (1.3 cm) on the other edge of the hem band, fold it over to the front to make a band, and topstitch it over the previous seam.

8

Fold the pillowcase in half, right sides together. Sew the long side seam and the end opposite the band with a ½" (1.3 cm) seam. Trim the seam. Zigzag or serge the seam allowances together to prevent raveling. Turn the pillow case right side out and press.

*Fabric: Tidings and Tales by J. Wecker-Frisch
Licensed to Wilmington Prints*

Susan Suggests

Tuck a piece of lace or folded strip of fabric into the seam when you topstitch the band of the pillowcase for a special accent.

shaving cream marbling

The craft of marbling paper originated in China more than 2,000 years ago.

Marbled paper became popular in seventeenth-century Europe as a decorative finish on book covers. Paper marbling required working with a vat of a thick seaweed medium on which paint was suspended. The paint was combed to make patterns and then carefully picked up by placing a piece of paper over it. As you can imagine, there are lots of ways the process can go wrong. Here you will use foamy shaving cream for a suspension medium and drop thin paint onto the surface. Instead of paper, you will use fabric to create a unique cloth for your next project.

materials and tools

Plastic cover for the table

Foamy shaving cream

Flat plastic surface

Plastic ruler

Transparent fabric paint:
Dye-na-Flow, assorted colors

Pipette or eyedropper

Coarse comb or hair pick

Fabric: white cotton or silk

Iron

shaving cream marbling

Toilette equipment has never been so glamorous! Shaving cream and combs combine to make the easiest marbled fabric ever.

Preparation
Protect your work surface with the plastic cover.

1

Spread enough shaving cream on the plastic surface, 1" (2.5 cm) deep, to match the size of your fabric. Smooth the top with the ruler—the top does not need to be level, just smooth.

2

Dribble straight lines of transparent paint onto the surface of the foam with a pipette or eyedropper. Use as many colors as you like.

3

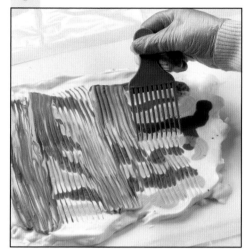

Starting at one side, comb across the lines of paint, moving from the top edge to the bottom. Wipe any shaving cream off the comb. Place the comb next to the already combed area and comb from the bottom to top. Keep reversing direction as you create your design.

4

Drape a piece of fabric face down onto the surface of the foam. Press it very gently into the foam so the paint adheres to the fabric. Carefully lift the fabric off the foam and scrape the excess foam from the fabric using the ruler. Comb through the paint left on the foam and make more prints until the foam is used up, adding more paint as needed. Let the paint dry and then iron to set. Rinse and dry the fabric pieces to remove the shaving cream.

Susan Suggests

You can also comb your marbling design in a curve or a series of curves for variety.

color discharge with bleach

It is just as much fun to take the color out of fabric as to put it in!

Simple techniques for applying bleach to black or dark-colored fabric give you dramatic results. Be sure your fabrics are cotton or rayon, as bleach will dissolve silk. Doing a few swatches on various black fabrics before you start will determine what colors you will get. Different fabrics give surprisingly different shades of brown, tan, red, and green. You will need to work in a well-ventilated area, label your bottles and buckets, neutralize the bleach in the discharged fabrics, and wear rubber gloves when using liquid bleach. Do not use bleach if you have breathing problems or are pregnant.

materials and tools

Plastic cover for the table

Neutralizing powder: Anti-Chlor

Water

Bucket or small basin

Fabric: cotton or rayon, black

Cheesecloth

Spray bottle

Liquid bleach, fresh bottle

Rubber gloves

Lightweight cardboard

Iron

Freezer paper

Clorox Bleach Pen Gel

Stencil (optional)

Sun Light dishwasher gel

Acrylic scrap for a palette

Rubber brayer or wooden paint mixing stick

Stamps: rubber or foam, with simple, bold designs

color discharge with bleach

A variety of bleaching products and **application methods offer myriad** variations for discharging, or removing color.

Preparation

Protect your work surface with the plastic cover. Before proceeding with any of the steps, prepare the neutralizing solution so you can stop the bleaching action immediately when your fabric attains the color you want. Mix a tablespoon (15 ml) of Anti-Chlor per gallon (4 l) of water. Before you begin, read through all of the techniques described in this section. One technique may contain a detailed instruction that is necessary for related techniques.

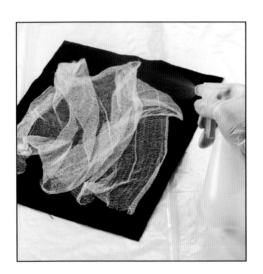

Misted Abstract Motifs

Lay the fabric on the table. Drape the cheesecloth on top of the fabric, creating creases and uneven edges. Use your hand to flatten the cheesecloth into the fabric. Fill the spray bottle with one part bleach and one part water. Spray over the cheesecloth and allow the fabric to rest until the color has changed around the edges. Don the rubber gloves and submerge the fabric and cheesecloth in the bucket of neutralizing solution to stop the bleaching action.

Designs with an Edge

Tear the edge of the cardboard into a wavy design. Place the torn edge near the top of the fabric and spray bleach water along the cardboard. Move the cardboard and spray along its edge again. Repeat until you get to the bottom of the fabric. Let the bleach work until you like the color, then don the rubber gloves and submerge the fabric in the bucket of neutralizing solution to stop the bleaching action.

Doodle Bleaching

Iron freezer paper, shiny side down, to the back of the fabric. This will stabilize it while you draw designs with a bleach pen. You can use a stencil, write words, or make abstract lines. Make sure you keep consistent pressure on the pen to avoid getting "exploding bubbles" in the stream of gel. Let the gel work until you like the color. Remove the freezer paper, don the rubber gloves, and submerge the fabric in the bucket of neutralizing solution to stop the bleaching action.

Gel Stamping

Pour dishwasher gel onto your palette and smooth it out with the brayer or wooden stick. Dab a foam or rubber stamp into the gel, then stamp the fabric. Let the gel work until you like the color, then don the rubber gloves and submerge the fabric in the bucket of neutralizing solution to stop the bleaching action.

Finishing

After the bleach is neutralized, wash the fabric in warm, soapy water and rinse.

Susan Suggests

When deciding when to neutralize your bleached pieces, remember that colors look darker on wet fabrics.

discharged dye pillow

A fun technique to try is discharging dye, which removes color rather than adding it.

It can be done with a variety of products using many different applications of the chemicals. Be sure to work in a well-ventilated area or outside. It is common to work with black fabric, but other colors also work well. Batiks, with their multiple layers of dye, produce wonderful results. For this project, you will apply a paste that can be used on all fibers, unlike bleach, and can be used with fewer precautions than chlorine. The color is removed with an iron through an almost magical process.

materials and tools

plastic cover for the table

rotary cutter, acrylic ruler, and mat

fabric: ½ yd. (0.5 m) of cotton batik

iron

stencil with large open areas (some of the discharge paste will seep under the stencil, so choose one without fine details)

sponge brush: 1" (2.5 cm)

discharge paste by Jacquard

batting: 13" (33 cm) square

backing fabric: 13" (33 cm) square

sewing machine

thread

pillow fabric: ½ yd. (0.5 m) of heavier weight coordinating homespun, corduroy, or silk matka

pins

16" (40.5 cm) square pillow form

discharged dye pillow (continued)

5

Place the batting and backing piece behind the batik fabric and, with a sewing machine, quilt around the stenciled motif to add dimension and strengthen the batik. This will also make the weight of the panel more comparable to the weight of the main pillow fabric.

6

Sew the two 2½" x 12½" (6.5 x 32 cm) strips of the main pillow fabric to the top and bottom edges of the batik panel with a ¼" (6 mm) seam allowance. Press the seams away from the center. Sew the two 2½" x 16½" (6.5 x 42 cm) strips of pillow fabric to the sides of the batik panel. Press the seams away from the center.

7

Turn under one long edge of a back panel piece ¼" (6 mm) and press. Turn under again 1" (2.5 cm), press, and stitch. Hem one long edge of the other panel in the same way. Place the pillow top right side up on the table and place the two backing pieces, right sides down and overlapped, onto the pillow top, so the raw edges match. Mark the corners of the backing pieces so they are rounded. Pin the edges and sew a ½" (1.3 cm) seam all the way around. Trim the corners. Turn the pillow right side out and insert the pillow form.

More Ideas

Apply the discharge paste to a foam stamp and stamp it onto the fabric. Or simply brush the discharge paste onto the fabric using a foam brush. Use masking tape to make a resist of straight lines. Use the discharged fabric for simple potholders or a pocket for a tote.

Susan Suggests

If you want more precise edges in your stenciling, spray stencil adhesive on the back of the stencil and let it dry. The tackiness of the adhesive will help hold the stencil in place on the fabric. Alternatively, make your stencil from freezer paper and iron it onto the fabric temporarily.

Earth Whispers

The earth whispers to every listening ear...
through leaves, grass, wind, and rain.
Peace found in things always here,
Wisdom found in ageless forms,
New life springing forth again and again.
Do you hear?

image to fabric sheet transfer

Transferring your favorite photographs to fabric is very fast and easy.

Printable fabric sheets are available in cotton and silk and even in silk organza for transparent layering. The sheets vary in price, but all work the same way—the main difference is their washability. If you want your project to be washable, test-wash and dry a sheet of the product you choose.

With your computer printer, a scanner, or an inexpensive color copier, fabric can be printed with digital photos, scanned children's artwork, photocopied real-life objects, or images sent to you by e-mail.

Then enjoy creating lovely items with your personally printed fabric. Scatter fabric-printed flower images among other pieces of a patchwork quilt, blend a printed landscape scene into a pieced or appliquéd frame, or put your own face onto an art doll to reveal your hidden persona!

materials and tools

Plain, white paper

Computer printer, scanner, and/or color copier

Objects to place on the copier: flowers, leaves, or children's artwork

Printed images or word-processed documents

Prepared fabric sheets for inkjet printing or photocopying

Sheer fusible web: Misty-white Fuse

Cooking parchment (available at grocery stores) or press sheet

Iron

image to fabric sheet transfer

Print words or images onto **treated fabric using your** ink-jet printer or copier.

Preparation

Before you begin, read through all of the techniques described in this section. One technique may contain a detailed instruction that is necessary for related techniques.

Preparing to Scan or Copy

As some machines print on the top and some on bottom side of the paper, draw an X on a test sheet of plain paper and put it through the copier or printer to determine which way to feed the fabric sheets. Collect all the materials needed to compose an image to scan or copy. If you want separate images of flowers or family photographs, arrange small ones on the copier or scanner so you can copy or print three or four images on one fabric sheet. To easily create a collage of items, compose and adhere them to a piece of paper and then place it face down on the scanner or copier.

Words Over Images

Print or copy a full-color image to a cotton fabric sheet and a poem or other writing to a transparent organza fabric sheet. Your image will remain bright even though it will be beneath the organza.

Images Over Words

Print or copy a poem or other writing to a cotton fabric sheet and a full-color image to a transparent organza fabric sheet. The words will still be distinct and the image will become muted and subtle.

Finishing

Cut a piece of fusible web to the size of your fabric sheets. Place the web over the cotton sheet and then place the organza sheet on top. Cover with parchment or a press sheet and fuse the three layers together using an iron.

Susan Suggests

Try printing black-and-white clip art on a fabric sheet and tinting the art with fabric paints before fusing organza over it.

photo-transfer mail sorter

Make a fun mail sorter for the front hall or kitchen, so each member of the family has a personal pocket.

Photo-transfer sheets—paper-backed fabric coated to make inkjet printing permanent—go right into the computer printer or copy machine. Use any printed or digital photo you have to make the centerpiece for each crazy-pieced block. Then assemble them into a wall hanging. Make one for your own family and everyone on your gift list.

materials and tools

Note: The sample is made for a six-person family; adjust the size for your own situation.

rotary cutter, acrylic ruler, and mat

fabric for front, pocket linings, and back: 1⅞ yd. (1.75 m)

six to eight pieces of coordinating prints for piecing: ¼ yd. (0.25 m)

binding fabric: ⅓ yd. (0.32 m)

double-stick tape

photos

copy paper

inkjet-photo fabric sheets: Inkjet Printing by Jacquard

copier

computer and inkjet printer (optional)

sewing machine

thread

iron

scissors

batting: 9½" x 63½" (24 x 161 cm), fusible cotton/polyester

pins

hanging stick

semitransparent inkjet fabric sheets: ExtravOrganza by Jacquard (optional)

fusible web: Mistyfuse (for ExtravOrganza)

photo-transfer mail sorter

1

With a rotary cutter, ruler, and mat, measure and cut a foundation for the pocket section from the main fabric 9½" x 63½" (24 x 161 cm).

Note: Cut the main fabric on the lengthwise grain. Cut two border pieces 2½" x 63½" (6.4 x 161 cm). For the back, cut one piece of the main fabric 13½" x 63½" (34.3 x 161 cm). Cut one 9½" (24 cm) square of lining fabric for each member of the family. Cut the piecing fabrics into 2" (5 cm)-wide strips as you need them. Cut the binding fabric into four 2" (5 cm)-wide strips.

2

Double-stick tape your photos to sheets of copy paper with space between the pictures. Place the sheets on the copier. Place the photo-transfer fabric, one sheet at a time, in the paper feed of the copier so the photos will print onto the fabric side. Print a sheet of fabric for each page of photos. Let dry. Follow the package directions if washing is needed.

3

Remove the paper backing from the fabric sheets and cut them apart so you have white space around each photo. Sew one strip of fabric to the side of one photo, right sides together, using a ¼" (6 mm) seam and angling the strip. Press the strip away from the photo. Trim off the excess strip with scissors.

4

Continue to add strips at an angle to the photo, pressing the strips away from the photo, and trimming off the end of each strip as you go around the photo. Add strips until the block is more than 9½" (24 cm) square. Trim it to an exact 9½" (24 cm). Repeat for all the photos.

Continued

5

Place a lining square, right sides together, with each pieced square and sew across the top and bottom edges with a ¼" (6 mm) seam allowance. Turn right side out and press the seams to one side, and then turn the lining to the back and press flat.

6

Steam-fuse the backing to one side of the batting and steam-fuse the center panel of main fabric to the middle of the batting on the other side.

7

Lay the top pocket on the fabric 2¼" (5.5 cm) from the top edge of the center panel. Pin through all the layers. Continue to pin the pockets to the hanging 1" (2.5 cm) apart until you reach the bottom. There should be 2¼" (5.5 cm) left at the bottom. Topstitch across the bottoms of the pockets through all the layers.

8

Pin the border strips right sides together over the raw edges of the center piece and pockets. Sew through all the layers with a ¼" (6 mm) seam. Press the borders away from the pockets onto the batting. Bind the edges, add a casing on the back, insert the hanging stick, and hang.

Susan Suggests

If you want to add names to each pocket, use semitransparent ExtravOrganza photo transfer fabric to make labels on your computer. Back the organza with Mistyfuse fusible web, and iron onto the pockets.

printout to fabric transfer

Who knew we would be using so much modern technology to create art?

If you have access to a laser or inkjet printer and an inkjet copier, you have the ability to print words and images on fabric without the expense of photo-transfer fabric sheets. When you use the one-step transfer method, you get a very subtle image. The inkjet and gel medium method is bolder—but messier! Sometimes painting over a transfer may smear some inkjet inks, so do a test run if neatness is a concern. For both methods, you can use a colored fabric.

materials and tools

Plastic cover for the table

Copyright-free images

Laser printer

Plain, white paper

Fabric: smooth-surfaced, white or light-colored

Iron

Inkjet printer or copier

Inkjet printer transparency sheet

Bristle brush with stiff, fine bristles

Gel medium: Golden Artist Colors Gel Mediums Regular Gel, matte

printout to fabric transfer

Quickly transfer an image with a laser printout, or use the equally quick three-step method using gel medium.

Preparation

Protect your work surface with the plastic cover. Before you begin, read through all of the techniques described in this section. One technique may contain a detailed instruction that is necessary for related techniques.

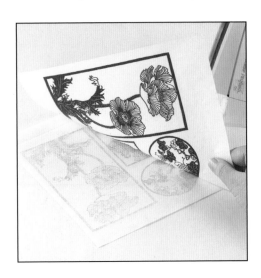

One-Step Laser Print Transfer

Make a black-and-white laser printout on plain paper. Turn it face down on white or light-colored fabric and iron the back of the paper for a couple of minutes on a hard surface. Lift a corner to check if the toner has transferred to the fabric. When it's ready, peel the paper off the fabric.

Inkjet Print an Image

Make an inkjet image on the rough side of a transparency sheet; both color and black-and-white images work well. If you don't know how the paper feeds into your printer or copier, draw an X on one side of a piece of paper and run it through to check. You can put several images on one sheet of transparency and then cut them apart.

Apply Gel Medium

Brush gel medium quickly and evenly, in both directions, onto the fabric. Extend the coverage slightly beyond the area the printed image will cover. Avoid getting the fabric too wet or the transparency will slide around and smear.

Transfer the Image

Place the transparency face down on the wet gel medium. Burnish the image with your fingernail, using circular strokes and pressing firmly. Make sure you burnish all areas. Lift a corner of the transparency to see if the image has transferred fully, and then slowly lift the transparency off the fabric. The image may not be perfect, especially if you missed an area when rubbing, but I like the "antiqued" look better anyway.

Note: Dover books are a very good source for copyright-free designs. Printed images are from *Authentic Chinese Cut-Paper Designs*, edited by Carol Belanger Grafton, part of the Dover Design Library.

Susan Suggests

If you want a darker laser-printed image, go to a copy shop and ask them to make a copy or printout using extra toner.

inkjet transparency to book cover

Use a copyright-free image, a favorite photograph, or one of your own drawings to decorate a removable album cover.

Use any inkjet copier or computer printer to make a transparency, and then burnish the ink onto fabric that's been painted with gel medium. The resulting image will be slightly distressed and is a nice alternative to the perfect look of a photo transfer done directly onto fabric. This method should be used on projects that will not be washed.

materials and tools

images: copyright-free images, photographs, drawings, or text

inkjet copier or computer printer

inkjet transparency sheets (available at office supply stores)

plastic cover for the table

tape

small piece of fabric for background of transfer

paint brush

gel medium: Golden regular gel, matte finish (available at art supply stores)

bone folder (optional)

iron and press cloth

three-ring binder or book to cover

measuring tape or ruler

scissors

cover fabrics: ½ yd. (0.5 m) each for outside and inside of book cover

sewing machine

thread

pins

embellishments (optional)

fusible quilt batting (optional)

inkjet transparency to book cover

Preparation
Cover your work surface with plastic.

 1

Look for an image that will fit nicely on the size book you wish to cover. Dover books are excellent sources for copyright-free images and can be found at any bookstore. To start, choose a small to medium-size design so you can practice transferring all the lines to the fabric before the gel medium dries out. You can place several small images on one transparency and cut them apart if you like. Make the inkjet copy or printout on the rough side of the inkjet transparency sheet.

2

Tape the background fabric to the plastic-covered work surface. With a brush, spread gel medium onto your background fabric quickly and evenly, brushing in both directions. Make sure the area covered is larger than your image. The fabric should be wet but not overly so, or the transparency will slip and the image will smear. Run your finger over the fabric to check for places that are not covered.

3

Place the transparency facedown on top of the wet gel medium and burnish the image onto the fabric with a bone folder or your fingernail. Use circular motions and be sure to cover every area, working quickly while the medium is still wet. Check to see the results by carefully lifting a corner. You won't get a perfect transfer, but that is the beauty of this method. Remove the transparency sheet, which should have very little ink left on it, and let the medium dry completely. Turn the dry transfer right side down on a press cloth and iron from the back to flatten it.

4

Measure the binder or other book when it is opened up and laid flat. Add 1" (2.5 cm) to the width and length for ease and seams. Decide how big to make your transfer piece and trim it to that size, adding ¼" (6 mm) seam allowances on all sides. Cut pieces of the outside cover fabric to border the transfer so it will be centered on the front of the cover and go around the back cover, adding extra to the size of the border pieces for seams and optional quilting.

Tip: Make a rough sketch of the pieces to cut so you can check your measurements.

Continued

5

Sew the outside cover pieces to the four sides of the transfer piece with ¼" (6 mm) seams, pressing the seam allowances away from the transfer. Add any embellishments at this point. You may wish to add batting and quilt the outer cover. Trim it to the size determined in step 4.

6

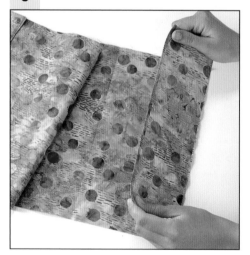

Cut a lining piece the same size as the outside cover and two lining pieces the height of the cover by 4" (10 cm) wide. Sew under ¼" (6 mm) on one long side of the two lining pieces. Lay the two strips right side up on the right side of the lining, with the hemmed edges toward the center.

7

Lay the outer cover right side down over the lining and strips. Pin. Sew a ¼" (6 mm) seam around the edges, leaving a 3" (7.5 cm) opening in the stitching on the bottom edge of the back section. Press under the seam allowances of the opening and clip the corners.

8

Turn the cover right side out through the opening and stitch or fuse the opening closed. Press the book cover, lay it flat, and insert the binder or sketchbook into the flaps.

Susan Suggests

Embellishments you might consider: fabric foil, piping around the transfer piece, beading, collage, rubber-stamping, or Paintstiks. Fusible batting makes it easy to quilt the outside cover without adding another piece of fabric on the back.

TEXTURE
and
DEPTH

foiling four ways

A bit of shine on a project propels it from flat to fabulous.

You can add foil to a project surface anytime during construction. All you need is foil, an iron, and an adhesive—a liquid, a granulated product, or a fusible web all work. For a unique look, make a dimensional foil appliqué with stick glue and your glue gun.

Foil comes in a variety of colors and in holographic designs. It may be packaged either as an assortment of small sheets or in 1-yard (0.9 m) lengths. New sheets give solid, bright shine. When the sheets start to wear out, they get even better because you can use several colors in succession for a softer, more complex look.

materials and tools

Plastic cover for the table

Foam brush: 1" (2.5 cm)

Foil adhesive

Stamp: rubber, acrylic, wood, or foam, with a bold, deep design

Fabric

Foil: various colors

Iron

Fusible web: Wonder-Under Transfer Web

Cooking parchment
(available at grocery stores)

Granulated adhesive:
Bo-Nash 007 Bonding Agent

Glue gun

foiling four ways

Foiled again!
Four times for four distinct looks.

Preparation

Protect your work surface with the plastic cover. Before you begin, read through all of the techniques described in this section. One technique may contain a detailed instruction that is necessary for related techniques.

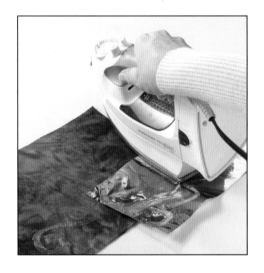

Direct to Fabric Foil Stamping

Brush foil adhesive onto the stamp. Try to get an even coat on the stamp but don't worry about a little excess on the edges. Stamp the adhesive onto your fabric and let it dry completely (two hours to overnight). Place a foil sheet over the dry adhesive, color side up. Set a dry iron to medium-high. Turn the iron slightly to its side and burnish the foil sheet three or four times with the edge. If the foil sheet starts to melt, turn the temperature down. Allow the foil to cool, then peel the sheet off the adhesive.

Shaped Foil

Cut a shape out of the fusible web. Iron the shape onto the fabric and remove the release paper. Place a foil sheet over the web, color side up, and burnish with the edge of the iron three or four times.

Note: Protect any previously applied foil from direct contact with the iron with parchment paper.

Star Dusting with Foil

Sprinkle granulated adhesive onto the fabric. Cover with a piece of parchment and iron until the granules melt onto the fabric. Remove the parchment, cover the melted granules with a foil sheet, color side up, and burnish with the edge of the iron. Protect all previously foiled areas with parchment.

Dimensional Foiling

Place a foil sheet, dull side up, on a heat-resistant ironing board. Heat a glue gun and then draw a shape with the glue on the foil sheet. Allow the glue to cool completely and then peel it off the foil. To attach the shape to fabric, place it glue side up on the ironing board. Place the fabric, wrong side up, over the shape and lightly press until the shape adheres to the fabric.

Susan Suggests

Hand-wash foiled fabrics; do not dry-clean.

fabric beads

Fabric beads make a fabulous closure on a garment, but think of using them in a necklace or on a wall hanging!

Place them in a pictorial piece as sculptural elements, as flower stems, as the parts of a chair, or as fence rails.

Discover how to create your own beads out of fabric that coordinates with your projects—without an expensive trip to the bead store.

Craft your beads in different shapes, decorate them with threads and trim or even other beads, foil them to add shine, and make them from fabrics that ravel in an interesting way. They are so quick and easy to create, you'll want to make lots.

Using the following method, you'll make sturdy beads that won't flatten out. If they will receive extra hard wear, coat them with polyurethane to seal them.

Sew finished beads to your background fabric or glue them down with permanent fabric adhesive.

materials and tools

Iron

Fusible web: Wonder-Under Transfer Web

Fabric: small pieces, include cotton batik and dupioni silk

Bamboo skewer

Decorative threads and yarns

Sponge brush: 1" (2.5 cm)

Foil adhesive

Foil: various colors

Sewing needle and thread

Permanent fabric adhesive: Fabri-Tac

fabric beads

Discover a quartet of ways
to create beautiful beads.

Preparation

Before you begin, read through all of the techniques described in this section. One technique may contain a detailed instruction that is necessary for related techniques.

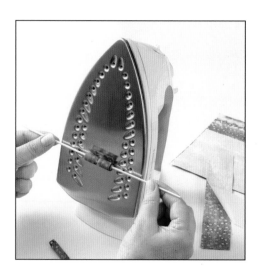

Cylinder Beads

Iron fusible web onto the back of fabric. Cut the fabric into strips that are the width of the bead you want, usually 1" to 1½" (2.5 to 3.8 cm) wide by 8" to 10" (20.3 to 25.4 cm) long. Remove the release paper from the fusible web and roll the fabric strip onto a bamboo skewer. Roll the skewered bead on an iron set to the proper temperature for the fabric, to fuse the fabric layers together. Don't roll too long, or you may fuse the bead onto the skewer permanently.

Tapered Beads

This technique works especially well with batik fabric or other hand-dyed fabrics that have scattered colors. Iron fusible web onto the back of fabric. Cut the fabric into strips as in "Cylinder Beads." Cut one end of each strip into a long, centered point. Remove the release paper from the fusible web and roll a strip onto the skewer, starting at the wide end. Melt the fabric layers together on the hot iron.

Decorative Touches

Decorate your beads with eyelet trim, thin yarn, narrow silk ribbon, or metallic thread. Lay the trim across one side of the bead. Wind it up the bead and back to the start of the trim. Tie the two ends together in a knot and let the tails dangle. Brush foil adhesive onto a bead and apply foil after it dries. (See "Direct to Fabric Foil Stamping" on page 18 for a description of this technique.)

Frayed Beads

To create a dupioni silk tapered bead, apply permanent fabric adhesive only to the pointed tip of the fabric, on the back side. This will secure the rolled layers, and the unglued edges will create an attractively raveled, soft bead. Think of all the possible variations!

Susan Suggests

Add further interest by wrapping a colored wire around your beads, or go for extra glitz by threading seed beads onto a wire and then wrapping the bead.

fabric bead necklace

Can't afford diamonds? Make a necklace every bit as exciting out of fabric you probably have in your stash.

Now you can have matching accessories for every outfit in your closet. There are all sorts of ways to embellish your beads and no end to the colors and styles you can make. Remember that you can also use fabric beads for garment closures, purse latches, tassels on scarves, three-dimensional elements on collages, and any number of other uses.

materials and tools

rotary cutter, acrylic ruler, and mat

fabrics: ½ yd. (0.5 m) tight weave and saturated color (batiks work well)

iron

fusible web: 1⅛ yd. (1 m) Wonder-Under

bamboo skewer

leather or rattail cord: 2⅓ yd. (2.1 m)

foil adhesive

cotton swab

foil for fabric

decorative yarns or trims

embellishments: wire and glass beads

silk dupioni

fabric glue

mixed media: felt or wooden beads, charms, or ribbons

fabric bead necklace

1

Using a rotary cutter, ruler, and mat, measure and cut the fabrics into four 10" x 17" (25 x 43 cm) pieces. Fuse Wonder-Under fusible web to the back of each piece, using a dry iron.

2

Cut 33 strips 1½" (3.8 cm) wide and 10" (25 cm) long. Cut the strips into long triangles, centering the point at one end and angling to the corners of the opposite end. Remove the fusible web release paper from the back of the strips.

3

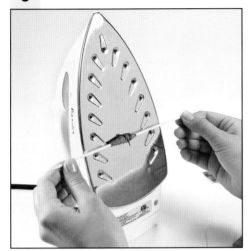

Lay a strip, fusible side up, on the work surface. Starting at the wide end, roll the strip on a bamboo skewer, ending with the narrow point. Hold the bead against a hot iron and roll it to melt the fusible web, making sure you catch the point securely. Heat the bead until it is firm, but do not melt the bead to the skewer. When cool, slide the bead off the skewer.

4

Repeat step 3 for all the fabric strips. Cut three lengths of cord to 24" (61 cm), 28" (71 cm), and 32" (81 cm). String nine beads on the short cord, eleven beads on the middle cord, and thirteen beads on the long cord. Tie all of the ends together in a square knot; the strands will fall in a cascade.

Continued

Foil

If you want to add a little glitz, leave the bead on the skewer and apply dabs of foil adhesive to the surface of the bead with a cotton swab. Stick the point of the skewer into something and allow the adhesive to dry. Then, place a piece of fabric foil over the dry adhesive, color side up, and use the iron to burnish the foil onto the bead. Turn the bead and reposition the foil until all of the adhesive is covered. Glitter and glitter glue also work well.

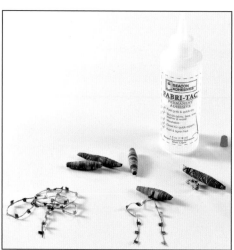

Embellish

Add interest and texture to your beads by winding them with yarns and trims. You may want to add a tiny bead of glue to the knot if the trim is slippery. Or wrap a piece of wire around the bead and add small glass beads to the wire ends.

Silk

Use dupioni silk to make lustrous, fringy beads for a dressy outfit. Do not back the fabric with fusible web because you want the edges to ravel. Simply cut the silk into long triangles, roll onto the skewer, and secure the points with fabric glue.

Mixed Media

Combine your fabric beads with felt or wooden beads, charms, or ribbons. Make the strips longer or wider for larger beads.

Susan Suggests

You could also string your beads onto yarn, fishing line, fine silver chain, or ball chain. If you choose to use ⅛" (3 mm) satin cord for stringing, make your beads using a chopstick or dowel rather than a skewer so the hole in the bead will accommodate the larger diameter cord.

silk fusion

Silk fusion, also called silk paper, consists of silk fiber that has not been spun into yarn or thread.

A textile medium, used as a soft adhesive, holds the fibers together. You may want to experiment with different mediums depending on the degree of stiffness you want for your final fabric.

Bombyx silk, from silkworms that eat mulberry leaves, is light, almost white in color, and quite smooth. The silkworms that produce tussah silk eat oak leaves and their silk is gold-colored (although it's often bleached) and coarser than bombyx. Either works well for silk fusion.

Add a variety of decorative elements to your fusion, or cut up the sheet and include the pieces in wool felting for a beautiful, tactile play of texture on texture. Of course, beading or other embellishments on the finished silk fusion add a fun touch and are easy to attach to the firm surface.

Use your silk fusion for wall hangings, containers such as boxes and bowls, book covers, and clothing.

materials and tools

Plastic cover for the table

Tulle or netting

Silk roving: bombyx or tussah, two or three colors

Decorative elements: ribbon, skeleton or silk leaves, or Angelina fibers

Shampoo without conditioner

Mixing container

Bristle brush: 1" (2.5 cm)

Paper towels

Textile medium

Screen or plastic mesh

silk fusion

Preparation
Protect your work surface with the plastic cover.

1

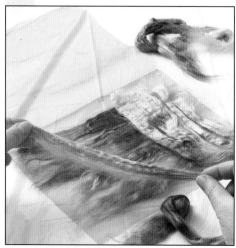

Lay out a piece of tulle or netting on your work surface. Pull small amounts of silk fiber from the hank of roving and lay them parallel to each other on half of the tulle in a thin and even layer.

Note: For the nicest look, never cut the silk roving. Hold your hands about 8" (20.3 cm) apart on the hank of roving and pull it apart.

2

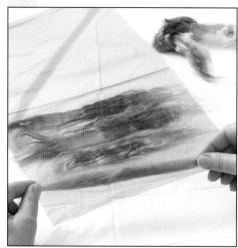

Lay additional fibers crosswise on top of the first layer. Lay a third layer of fibers in the direction of the first layer. Check for thin spots in the layers and fill in, if necessary.

3

Lay silk or skeleton leaves, ribbons, or other decorative elements on top of the third layer of fibers. Cover them with wisps of fibers to hold them in place. Fold the other half of the tulle over the top of the layered silk fibers and embellishments.

4

Dissolve about ½ teaspoon (2.5 ml) of shampoo into 2 cups (0.5 l) of water. Brush the solution on the tulle until all layers are thoroughly saturated. Blot out as much water as possible with paper towels. Coat both sides of the tulle with full-strength textile medium. Let the fusion dry on a screen or piece of plastic mesh and then peel it off the tulle.

Susan Suggests

Create thickness through additional layers. After completing a few projects, you will be able to judge how thick you want your silk fusion for its final use.

silk cocoons and more

Silk comes in wondrous forms, and now many of them are readily available to quilters and fabric artists.

No other fabric feels like silk or slurps color like silk.

Cocoons are the source of silk filament, and a dried worm is inside each one. Silk carrier rods are a by-product of the silk-making process and can be peeled into thin layers. Hankies are gossamer-thin layers of silk fiber that can be further peeled apart.

Use the cocoons, carrier rods, and hankies to make necklaces, tassels, and embellishments on wall hangings or for other creative projects.

materials and tools

Plastic cover for the table

Silk cocoons

Small scissors with a very sharp tip

Transparent fabric paint:
Dye-na-Flow, assorted colors

Container

Silk carrier rods

Hemostat or tweezers

Pipettes or eyedroppers

Paper towels

Silk hankies
(a form of silk, not a handkerchief)

Spray bottle containing water

Iron

Permanent fabric adhesive: Fabri-Tac

gossamer silk

Gossamer silk, unlike the stiffer silk fusion, remains soft and more like a fabric.

It can be used for scarves, vests, wall hangings, or fluttery window coverings. Gossamer silk is fairly sturdy because the sewing holds it together. It can be embellished either during the layering and sewing process or after the stabilizer is removed. Yarn, trim, or shapes cut from China silk, Angelina, or Mylar are just a few of the embel-lishments you can include as you lay out the fibers—just make sure your additions can withstand a bath in warm water. A bit of patience is needed when spreading out the silk and for stitching, but the results will get rave reviews.

materials and tools

Water-soluble stabilizer: Sulky Super Solvy

Hank of dyed silk top*

Embellishments: yarn, trim, or shapes of China silk, Angelina, or Mylar

Straight pins

Walking foot

Cotton thread to match the silk fiber

Sewing machine

Container of warm water to dissolve stabilizer

Paper towels or a terry towel

* This is processed silk fiber before it is spun into thread. Either tussah or bombyx silk will work.

gossamer silk

You'll work with soft silk fibers and embellishments **to create an interesting fabric** with a grid pattern in just four easy steps.

1

Lay out a piece of water-soluble stabilizer slightly larger than the size of the project you have planned. Pull apart (do not cut) the silk top, holding your hands about 8" (20.3 cm) apart on the hank and pulling.

2

Carefully lay out thin strands of the silk fiber on the stabilizer, making sure there are no thick clumps and that the stabilizer is covered completely. Place embellishments on top of the fibers. Add more silk, if you like, or leave the additions to be caught by the stitching.

3

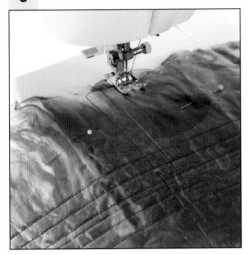

Cover the silk fiber with another piece of stabilizer and pin through all of the layers to hold the fibers and embellishments in place. Using a walking foot if you have one and cotton thread that matches the silk fiber, stitch through the layers in a ½" (1.3 cm) grid, starting with the horizontal and vertical lines in the middle (which will help hold everything in place while you do the rest of the stitching). Stitch the entire piece. It is not necessary to sew the stitching lines perfectly straight.

4

Soak the stitched piece in warm water for 5 to 10 minutes to dissolve the stabilizer. If you still feel stabilizer on the wet fabric or if the fabric is stiff after it dries, rinse it again. Spread the fabric out on paper towels or a terry towel, reshaping it to its original size. Let dry.

Note: Silk fiber dyed by Diane Bartels.

Susan Suggests

Try free-motion sewing for an organic look, making sure your stitching lines cross over each other to create a net of stitches. Be sure to start stitching in the center of your composition.

gossamer silk candle cover

Use a variation of the gossamer silk technique to decorate your home with a colorful and unique accessory.

Sewing the fibers to a piece of heat-resistant template plastic and adding other embellishments gives you a translucent cover for a candle. The light can be seen through the needle holes and the thin spots in the fiber. Make one version with lace and ribbon, another with a painted motif under the fibers, and a third with beaded trim along the top edge.

materials and tools

- plastic cover for the table

- measuring tape or ruler

- roving: silk, viscose, nylon, or other non-felting fibers in roving (combed, not loose) form

- templar heat-resistant template plastic

- embellishments: lace, ribbons, silk pieces, or artificial leaves and flowers

- scissors

- water-soluble stabilizer: Sulky Super Solvy

- sewing machine

- large sewing machine needle: Jeans #16

- cotton decorative thread

- darning foot (optional)

- sink or other container for water

- lace or beaded trim

- zipper foot

- strong glue: Fabri-Tac

- two or three large rubber bands

- two clothespins or clamps

- votive candles in aluminum holders

- rubber stamp

- paint: Jacquard Neopaque

- sponge brush: 1" (2.5 cm)

- iron

gossamer silk candle cover

Preparation
Cover your work surface with plastic.

1

Pull lengths of fiber from the silk skein about 11" (28 cm) long by holding your hands that far apart and pulling gently. Separate the fibers into thin wisps and lay them parallel over the surface of a piece of template plastic, keeping the layer thin so light will show through.

2

Lay lace, ribbons, silk leaves or flowers, or other trims onto the surface of the fibers. You can add a few more wisps of fiber if you like. Make sure all embellishments are colorfast in water, because you will be rinsing the candle cover to remove the stabilizer.

3

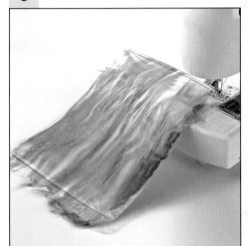

With scissors, cut a piece of Super Solvy slightly larger than the template plastic and lay it over the fibers, pressing out the air between the layers. Using the large sewing machine needle and decorative thread, sew along the shorter edges of the plastic to secure the Solvy and fiber ends.

Note: The fibers and embellishments will shift slightly as you work. Use a longer stitch length to prevent the plastic from tearing between stitches. Use sturdy cotton thread to add interest and withstand the heat of the candle.

4

Use a straight stitch to make a ½" (1.3 cm) grid of stitching or meander-stitch with a darning foot all over the surface of the fiber sandwich, catching all trims and fibers in the stitching. Trim the excess fiber and stabilizer from the edges.

Continued

5

Soak the fiber sandwich in warm water for 10 minutes, then drain the water and run water over the piece to remove all traces of the stabilizer, which will feel slippery if present. Blot with towels and allow to dry.

6

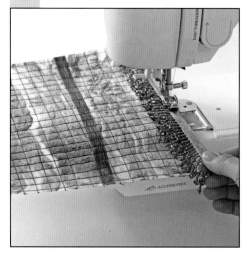

If you are using a beaded trim on the top edge, sew it on after the fibers are dry. Use a zipper foot so you can sew close to the beaded edge. Allow for a ½" (1.3 cm) overlap on one edge.

7

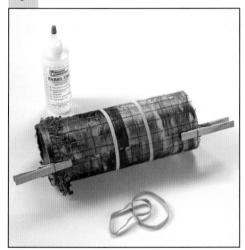

Overlap the edges of the template plastic ½" (1.3 cm) and glue in place. Place rubber bands around the middle and clamps at the ends of the candle cover while it dries to keep the overlap even and in contact with the underside edge. Remove the clamps and bands and place the finished cover over a votive candle.

8

For another look, rubber stamp a motif onto the template plastic using Jacquard Neopaque paint. With a sponge brush, dab paint onto the rubber stamp and stamp onto the plastic sheet. Let the paint dry thoroughly, iron the plastic from the back with a medium-hot iron to set the paint, and then layer the fibers over the painted motif as described in steps 1 to 5. Finish as in step 7.

Note: Hand-dyed silk and viscose roving by Diane Bartels.

Susan Suggests

Place the votive candle in its holder on a heatproof coaster to protect your table and light your candle cover all the way to the top.

burned-edge appliqué

Painting the silk, cutting rough shapes, and then burning the edges is a fun way to create artistic appliqués.

The singed, gray edges add a sophisticated verve to the fabric's colors. Appliqué by hand or with a sewing machine. If you stitch through the batting and backing fabric at the same time, you will complete the quilting process too! Be sure to use tweezers to hold the silk in the flame if you are doing small pieces. Have a container of water nearby in case the silk starts to burn too quickly.

Yvonne Porcella, in her book *Colors Changing Hue*, first introduced me to this method for sealing the edges of silk shapes so they could be appliquéd without turning under seam allowances.

materials and tools

Plastic cover for the table

Container with water

Scissors

Silk: natural color, 8–12 mm

Spray bottle with water

Transparent fabric paint:
Dye-na-Flow, assorted colors

Sponge brushes: 1" (2.5 cm)

Coarse salt

Iron

Votive candle in secure, heat-proof holder

Tweezers

Backing fabric:
9½" x 12" (24.1 x 30.5 cm)

Batting:
thin, 9½" x 12" (24.1 x 30.5 cm)

Pins (optional)

Sewing machine with darning foot

Thread to match appliqués

Glue stick

Note: Pins aren't needed if you use fusible batting.

burned-edge appliqué

Salt and flame—sounds like ingredients in a cookbook—but here is a recipe for softly textured, vibrantly colored silk.

Preparation

Protect your work surface with the plastic cover. Have the container of water ready is case the silk starts to burn too quickly.

1

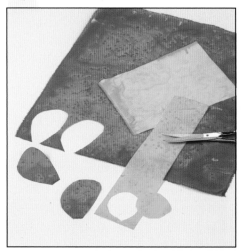

Cut several pieces of silk about 11" (27.9 cm) square and place them flat on the plastic-covered table. Spray the silk with water. Paint each piece a different color using a separate brush for each color. Spray with water again to make the paint run and puddle. Sprinkle coarse salt on the surface of the wet silk, and then let the fabric dry slowly. Remove the salt crystals and iron the silk to heat set the paint.

2

Prepare the appliqués and background pieces by cutting the painted silk into rough shapes slightly larger than you want the finished pieces to be. Don't worry about exact outlines because you will be burning the edges to get the final shape.

3

Light the candle. Using the tweezers, hold the edge of a cut silk piece horizontally in the side of the candle flame. Avoid holding the silk at the top of the flame, which will produce soot and ruin the colors. Let the silk burn just long enough to shape the piece. Rotate the piece until all the edges have been burned. The silk should stop burning as soon as you remove it from the flame, but if it continues, blow gently on it or dunk it in a container of water and try again after it dries. Keep the silk from touching the wax. Pull any crunchy bits off the edges, but avoid smearing soot onto the silk.

4

Place the backing fabric wrong side up and cover it with the batting. Position and then pin the background pieces of silk on the batting. Sew ⅛" (3 mm) from the edges of each silk piece through all the layers. Adhere the appliqué pieces to the background with the glue stick and topstitch around the edges. Cut the page to 8½" x 11" (21.6 x 27.9 cm) after stitching and finish the edges as you like.

Susan Suggests

You can use any natural-colored silk that has body. Perfect choices are China silk or silk twill of 8 to 12 mummie. (Mummie is the measure of weight for silk.)

burned-edge appliqué tea cozy

Make a pretty accessory for your table or sideboard with painted silk and burned-edge appliqué.

Dye-na-Flow paint makes it easy to add vibrant color without the complexity of dyeing, and it keeps the soft hand of the fabric. Since you are painting "blobs" on a large piece of fabric and then tearing it into strips, all of the colors blend. The blackened edges lend a nice contrast to the brightness of the silk. This technique could also be used for a lovely vest.

materials and tools

- plastic cover for the table

- fabric: ¾ yd. (0.7 m) of natural color 12 mm silk twill or other silk with body

- spray bottle filled with water

- paint: Dye-na-Flow by Jacquard

- sponge brushes: 1" (2.5 cm)

- silk salt or other coarse salt

- iron

- scissors

- batting: cotton/polyester

- sewing machine

- thread: to match cozy and invisible for appliqué

- walking foot

- pins

- candle in tip-proof holder

- large tweezers or forceps to hold silk in flame

- container of water to douse burning silk if it gets out of control

- darning foot

- lining fabric: ⅜ yd. (0.35 m), cotton

burned-edge appliqué tea cozy

Preparation
Cover your work surface with plastic.

1

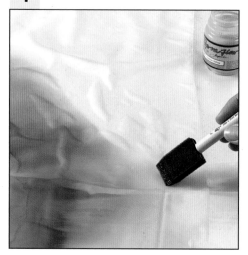

Tear the silk into one ½-yd. (0.5 m) and one ¼-yd. (0.25 m) piece. Lay the larger piece on the plastic-covered work surface and spray it with water. Brush on Dye-na-Flow paint with a sponge brush straight from the jar, or dilute the paint for a lighter look. Paint irregular areas of color rather than a pattern. To make the colors blend, make sure the silk is quite wet—spray it again after painting if you wish. Use colors that mix well, such as blue and yellow, red and blue, or red and yellow, or the three printer's primaries (magenta, turquoise, and yellow), as in the sample.

2

Sprinkle silk salt over the surface of the painted silk and allow it to dry undisturbed. Walk away and do something else because the process takes about 45 minutes to work. When you return, you will be amazed at how the salt has attracted the paint, making streaks and circles. Allow it to dry completely. Brush off the salt.

3

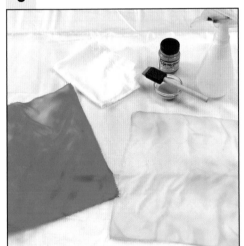

Tear the smaller silk piece into four 9" x 11" (23 x 28 cm) pieces. Lay out the pieces on the plastic and spray them with water. Paint two of them in shades of green for leaves; paint the other two in flower colors that contrast with your background piece. Allow them to dry. Iron all of the silk pieces for 30 seconds on each area to set the paint. Wash and dry the large piece to remove the salt residue and iron smooth.

4

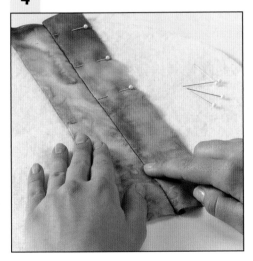

Draw a done-shaped pattern 14" (35.5 cm) wide and 11" (28 cm) tall. Use it to cut two pieces of batting. Tear the large piece of silk into strips about 2" (5 cm) wide. Place two silk strips right sides together in the middle of one batting piece and sew along one edge through all the layers with a ¼" (6 mm) seam allowance, using the cozy thread and a walking foot. Finger press the top strip over onto the batting and pin.

Continued

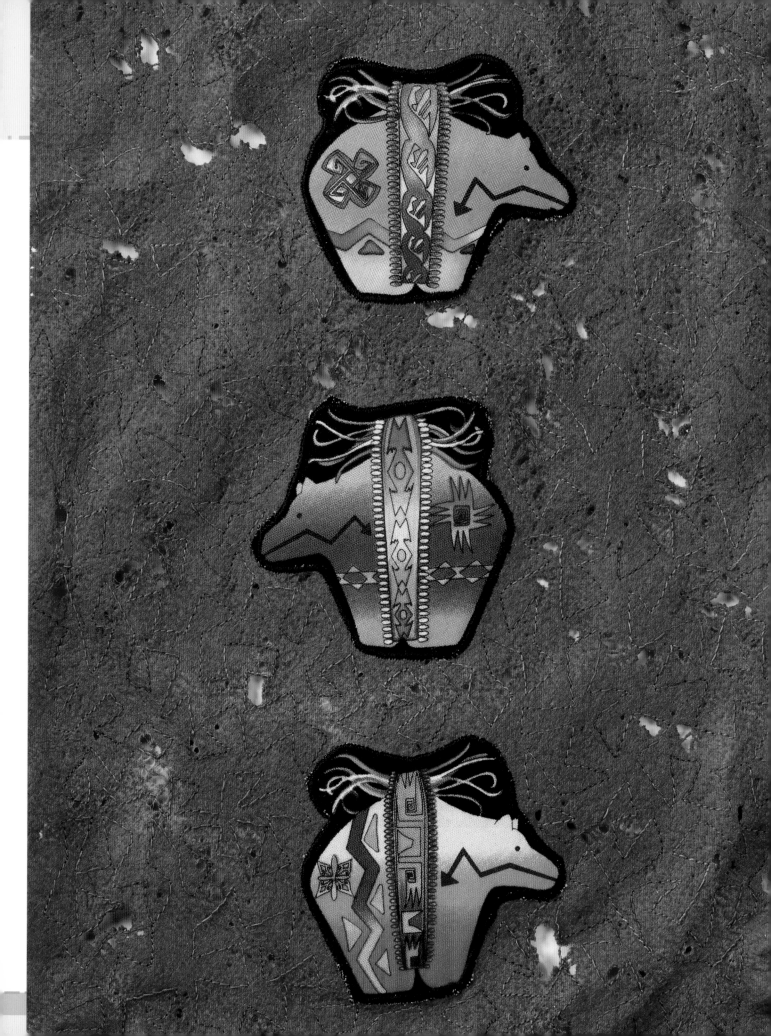

distressed felt

For those who are *really* adventurous, there are techniques in which you apply heat to fabrics to burn, melt, or distort them.

Soldering irons, changeable-tip heat tools, heat guns, regular irons, and hair dryers all are being used to alter fabric. Cotton or silk fabric that is applied to a synthetic fabric creates areas of resistance to the heat. You can also build up heavy concentrations of thread. On this project, synthetic felt was used with cotton appliqués and thread, and then a heat gun was used to melt and distress the felt creating holes and discolorations as well as shrinkage in the overall piece. Remember to do this outside or with proper ventilation, as the process will create fumes.

materials and tools

Iron

Fusible web: Wonder-Under Transfer Web

Fabric: cotton, with motifs

Synthetic felt: 9" x 12" (22.9 x 30.5 cm)

Sewing machine with satin stitch and darning feet

Cotton thread: matching and decorative

Heat gun

distressed felt

"Holey" moly! Heat and felt and fanciful fabric **turn into a lacy decorative accent** when put together in a few easy stages.

Iron fusible web to the back of the printed fabric, following the manufacturer's instructions. Cut out two or three motifs, leaving a generous ⅛" (3 mm) around the edge of each design.

Peel off the paper backing from the cutouts and fuse the motifs to synthetic felt. Do not worry if the felt starts to shrink from the heat of the iron.

3

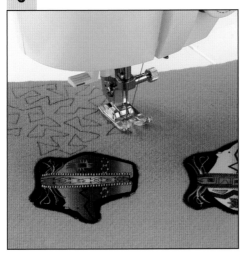

Satin stitch around the printed motifs with matching cotton thread. Set the machine for free motion stitching, drop the feed dogs, and change to decorative cotton thread. Stitch all over the background, using either a standard stippling design, triangular stippling like the sample, or loops. The stitching will hold the piece together when you melt the felt away.

4

Turn the piece over and heat over the entire piece with a heat gun held about 2" (5.1 cm) above the surface. The felt will start to shrink and discolor slightly. Keep heating the felt until holes start to appear. Turn the piece right side up and heat some more, trying to get holes and discoloration evenly spaced around the surface. You decide when the piece is finished—some people have hardly any felt left when they are done!

Susan Suggests

If you want significant changes in the character of your textile, use synthetic fabrics. Natural fibers tend to create ash when burned instead of melting or distorting.

painted fusible web

Fabric artists have adapted fusible web—which once simply hid between layers of fabric—into an art element.

This fine web of fusible adhesive can be painted and then used as an overlay, a background, or an appliqué.

Using a thin fabric paint to add color to the web while it remains on its paper backing causes the paper to crinkle, which adds pattern to the web. The decorative web can then be fused onto a piece of printed or solid-color fabric.

This technique is perfect for people who like serendipity in the final product because the web often releases from the paper backing unevenly.

materials and tools

Plastic cover for the table

Fusible web: Wonder-Under Transfer Web

Transparent fabric paint:
Dye-na-Flow, assorted colors

Sponge brushes: 1" (2.5 cm)

Hair dryer (optional)

Background fabric: high color contrast, such as black and white

Iron

Cooking parchment
(available at grocery stores)

Appliqué fabric: large motif

Granulated adhesive:
Bo-Nash 007 Bonding Agent

painted fusible web

Layers of paint and fabric combine to give dimension and breadth to a simple black-and-white print.

Preparation

Protect your work surface with the plastic cover.

1

Lay a piece of fusible web on the table, web side up. Cover the web with transparent paint, working quickly. Apply as many colors as you like, using a separate brush for each color. You may add water to the paint if you want a diffused effect. The paper backing will crinkle when it gets wet enough, so do not rework an area or you will flatten out the texture. Let the paint dry or speed up the process with a hair dryer.

2

Cut a piece of completely dry, painted fusible web to your chosen size. Place it web side down on the front of your background fabric, and iron over the paper backing for a few seconds. Make sure the edges are secure. Let cool and then peel the paper backing off of the web. Some areas of the web may stay on the paper backing, but that is part of the fun of this technique. Cover the fabric with parchment and press the web thoroughly into the fabric.

3

Cut a motif from the appliqué fabric. Place it on the background fabric. Protect all exposed web with parchment and press the appliqué thoroughly until it is secure.

Note: If an area under the appliqué lacks fusible web, sprinkle a little bonding agent on the fabric before heat setting.

4

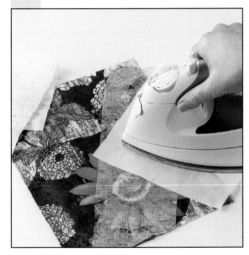

Cut a second piece of painted web (perhaps a piece that reflects a color from the appliqué) and iron it over the motif, being careful to protect any exposed web with parchment. Cover the motif completely or partially, as you prefer. Peel off the paper backing, cover with parchment, and press the web thoroughly into the fabric.

Susan Suggests

Once the painted web is ironed to the fabric, you can further embellish it with foil, ribbons, or other fibers because it still has adhesive properties.

Colorful Quilts
2233 Energy Park Dr.
St. Paul MN 55108

Art washes away
from the soul
the dust of
everyday life.

painted fusible web postcards

Everyone enjoys getting mail that is colorful,
creative, and fun.

These simple fabric postcards can be mailed with a first-class stamp. For a little extra postage, you can add an amazing amount of embellishment.

Make personal fabric postcards for all occasions and keep some on hand for quick greetings and gifts.

materials and tools

rotary cutter, acrylic ruler, and mat

fusible web: Mistyfuse

plastic sealable bag

measuring spoon

powdered pigments: Pearl Ex
by Jacquard

fabric: black and white print or
plain black

cooking parchment
(available at grocery stores)

iron

foil for fabric

very stiff interfacing: Timtex or Peltex

paper-backed fusible web:
Wonder-Under

embellishments: printed fabrics,
ribbons, silk leaves, lace, trims, buttons,
and beads

hand-sewing needle

netting (optional)

backing fabric: sturdy white cotton

rubber stamps (quotations work well)

ink pad

fabric pen

sewing machine

thread: variegated and white

painted fusible web postcards

1

With a rotary cutter, ruler, and mat, measure and cut a piece of Mistyfuse 7" (18 cm) wide. Place it in a large plastic sealable bag and add about ½ teaspoon of Pearl Ex powder. You may use more than one color, but they will blend rather than give two distinct colors when applied to the web. Close the bag and shake to distribute the pigment powder fairly evenly onto the web.

2

Cut a piece of fabric the same size as the painted Mistyfuse. Place the web over the fabric and cover with cooking parchment. Use a dry iron to press the web onto the fabric. Make sure the web is securely attached to the fabric so that the foil in the next step does not pull it off.

3

Place a piece of fabric foil, color side up, over the painted web. With the edge of a dry iron, rub over the foil sheet quickly three or four times to transfer the foil to the web. Light strokes will give you a better look than heavy ones. Leave some areas without foil for contrast.

4

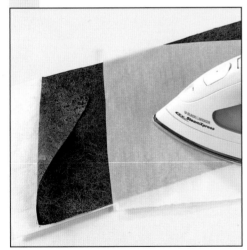

Cut a piece of stiff interfacing and a piece of paper-backed fusible web the size of the fabric. Using a dry iron, press the paper-backed fusible onto the interfacing, let cool, and pull off the backing paper. Iron the painted fabric onto the fusible web, using a piece of cooking parchment over the fabric to protect the iron. Cut the fabric/interfacing piece into four 4½" x 6½" (11.5 x16.5 cm) rectangles. You will trim them to their final size later.

Continued

5

Cut out motifs from printed fabrics or choose ribbons, silk leaves, skeleton leaves, lace, and trims that coordinate with the painted web, foil, and background fabric. Place the items on the postcards, cover with cooking parchment, and fuse in place. If the Pearl Ex and foil have exhausted the adhesive properties of the Mistyfuse, place another piece of web under the motifs, ribbons and so on.

6

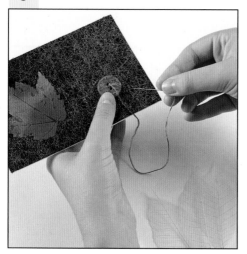

Trim the cards to an exact 4" x 6" (10 x 15 cm) rectangle (U.S. postal requirement). Do seed stitching by hand or add machine-stitched details. Sew embellishments such as buttons or beads to the postcards by hand or machine. Make sure that any decorations are very firmly attached to the cards. Even if you ask for hand cancellation at the post office, the cards will still go through various machines on the way to the recipient. One way to protect delicate embellishments is to cover the whole front of the card with netting.

7

Make four backs for the cards from sturdy white cotton cut 4½" x 6½" (11.5 x 16.5 cm). On the left side of the fabric, rubber stamp a quotation using ink or use a fabric pen to write a personal message and add your return address. On the right side of the backing piece, put the recipient's address. For postcard exchanges, I use photo transfer fabric sheets to print the return address multiple times and make a sheet of recipient's addresses, which can then be applied to the back of the card with fusible web when the postcard is completed.

8

Center a postcard front over a backing piece with wrong sides together. Set the machine for satin stitching and thread the machine with variegated thread on the top and white or variegated thread in the bobbin. Satin stitch the edge of the postcard and then trim off the excess backing fabric. Use a self-adhesive stamp on the back and burnish it onto the fabric securely with your fingernail. Drop your postcards into a mailbox and prepare for rave reviews!

Susan Suggests

Gather a group of friends and have a postcard exchange. Set a deadline and decide on a theme—otherwise, anything goes! One of the best exchanges I've been part of was based on dots. Imaginations ran wild with everything from yellow polka-dot bikinis to quilt pox to elegant dots made from satin.

angelina fiber

Angelina is different from any other fiber you've seen.

It melts together into a luminous flat sheet that can be used as created, cut into shapes, trapped behind netting, sewn as an appliqué, adhered to fabric with paint, fused to fabric, or embossed with stamps.

Create bowls and other vessels using it as a stand-alone material, or combine it with other fibers for felting or silk fusion. A highly reflective, polyester fiber, Angelina adds sparkle to water or sky even in minute amounts. For extra pizzazz, add threads, sequins, or bits of silk into the fiber before fusing. Experiment and have fun! This fiber opens many possibilities for you.

After creating a sheet of Angelina, try burning the edges or burning through it with a heat tool or candle flame. Pressing Angelina with an iron changes its color—a process you manage by controlling the heat. The more heat, time, and pressure you use when you iron the Angelina, the more the color changes. Be sure to always use a piece of cooking parchment over and under the fiber whenever applying heat.

materials and tools

Hot-fix fiber: Angelina

Cooking parchment
(available at grocery stores)

Iron

Stamp: rubber, acrylic, wood, or foam, with bold, deep design

Sheer fusible web: Misty-white Fuse

Fabric

angelina fiber

Angelina fiber offers four techniques
to use alone or layer
into one intriguing page.

Preparation

Before you begin, read through all of the techniques described in this section. One technique may contain a detailed instruction that is necessary for related techniques.

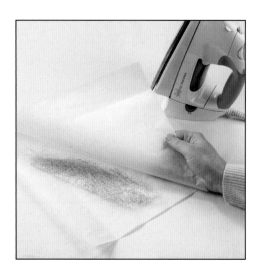

Fuse the Fibers

Place a thin layer of fibers on a piece of parchment. Cover them with another sheet of parchment. Set the iron to the temperature for silk and briefly press over the top of the parchment. Check the fibers to see if they are fused together and press a little longer if they are not. If the color changes more than you like, turn down the temperature of the iron and try again. Trim the edges of the fused piece if you desire.

Create a Stamp-Embossed Shape

Place a stamp right side up on the ironing surface. Arrange the fibers on top of the stamp. Put a piece of parchment on top of the fibers and iron for a few seconds. Check the fibers to see if the image of the stamp is embossed into the surface. To change the color of the image while leaving the surrounding fibers the original color, leave the iron on the stamp a little longer. Trimming the uncooked fibers off the edges is optional.

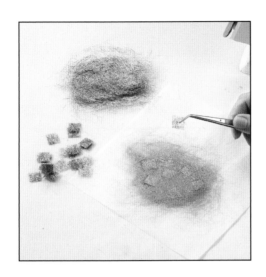

Make Shapes

Place a thin layer of fibers on a piece of parchment. Cover them with another sheet of parchment. Briefly melt the fibers into a sheet that barely holds together. Cut it into squares, triangles, or any shape you like. Place a layer of uncooked fibers in a contrasting color on a piece of parchment, arrange the shapes on top and cover with another very thin layer of the fibers. Cover with parchment and iron to fuse everything together.

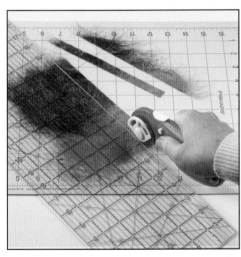

Form a Fusible Appliqué

Layer a piece of parchment, a 9" x 11½" (22.9 x 29.2 cm) piece of fusible web, fibers, and another piece of parchment, in that order. Iron to fuse the layers together, but stop before the colors change. Cut the fused-fiber sheet into strips. Weave the strips together on top of the piece of fabric. Cover the fibers with parchment. Carefully turn the fabric over and iron quickly from the back to fuse the fibers to the fabric.

Susan Suggests

Angelina is washable and fun to use on a garment. Additional heat applied to the fibers will continue to change their appearance, so hand-wash your garment and dry it flat.

A good resource for additional information is *Between the Sheets with Angelina* by Alysn Midgelow-Marsden.

angelina jar wrap

Angelina "hot fix" fibers are synthetic fibers that will fuse to each other when heat is applied.

They are very shiny, come in luscious colors, and can trap other fibers and embellishments when they are formed into a sheet. For a fun project, make a jar wrap and display flowers or other items in it or make a cone to hang. Be sure to protect your iron from touching the fiber and prepare to have a sparkly sewing room and clothing!

materials and tools

small canning jar or mayonnaise jar

tape measure

pencil

string

cooking parchment
(available at grocery stores)

fiber: Angelina "hot fix" in several colors
or one sampler pack

iron

scissors

embellishments: sequins, trims, fibers,
bits of silk

ribbon: several ⅛" (3 mm)-wide ribbons,
approximately ½ yd. (0.5 m) of each plus
some for snippets

stiff piece of paper: 8½" x 11"
(21.5 x 28 cm)

tape

clear-drying glue

angelina jar wrap

1

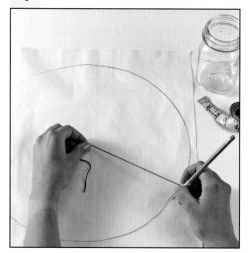

Measure your jar by running a tape measure down the side, across the bottom, and up the opposite side. Allow for 2" (5 cm) extra to make the ruffle around the top. I used a 14" (35.5 cm) circle. Draw a circle with your final measurement as the diameter onto a piece of cooking parchment, using a string taped onto a pencil as a compass. It does not have to be a perfect circle, because it will be used only as a pressing guide.

2

Pull apart the Angelina fiber and lay it out on the parchment paper in a thin layer, using as many colors as you wish. Make sure you cover the circle over the drawn lines and cross the fibers over each other. Too thick a layer will require too much heat to melt the fibers and the colors will change and dull.

3

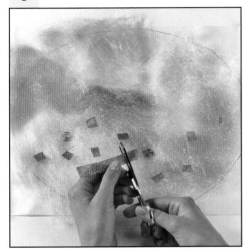

Make a small sheet of Angelina fiber in a contrasting color by using an iron to fuse it quickly between sheets of parchment paper. Cut it into small squares or other shapes. Distribute the sequins, trims, or cut-up bits of Angelina over the unmelted fiber.

4

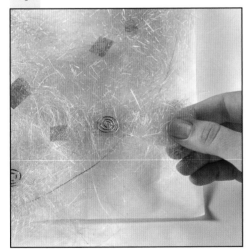

Add a small amount of Angelina fiber on top of the embellishments so they will be firmly caught in the Angelina sheet when it is melted.

Continued

angelina jar wrap (continued)

5

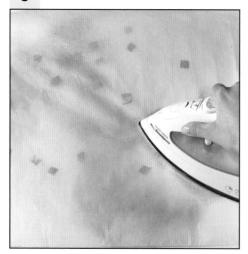

Cover the Angelina with another sheet of cooking parchment and heat the surface with an iron set for silk or wool (irons vary, so experiment with the temperature). The Angelina should fuse to itself and capture the other embellishments.

Note: The more time and pressure you put on the iron, the more the color of the Angelina will change. It is possible to turn the Angelina completely black, but it is more likely that you will just dull the color if you leave the heat on too long. Do some testing before you make your jar cover.

6

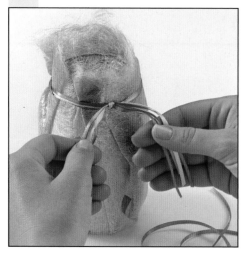

Place the jar in the center of the circle of fused Angelina, pull the sheet up around the jar, and tie the ribbon around the top of the jar. Use several narrow ribbons together for a different look, or use some of the exciting knitting ribbons and add charms to the ends.

1

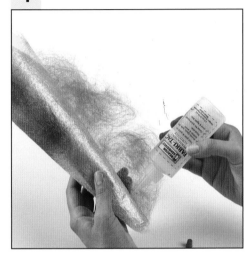

Angelina Cone

Make a pretty cone of Angelina to hang on a tree, decorate a window, or serve as a delightful party favor. Following the steps above, make a circle of Angelina fiber 12" (30.5 cm) in diameter or smaller. Make a cone of stiff paper and tape it together for a form. Wrap the fused circle of Angelina around the form and glue it along the edge.

2

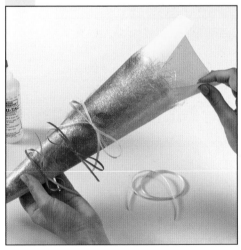

Wind the cone with ribbons and glue them in place. Make a hanger out of ribbon and glue it to the top of the cone. Add trims as desired, and then remove the paper form.

Susan Suggests

After it is fused into a sheet, Angelina fiber can be foiled, painted, burned along the edges, and further embellished. Spend a little time exploring!

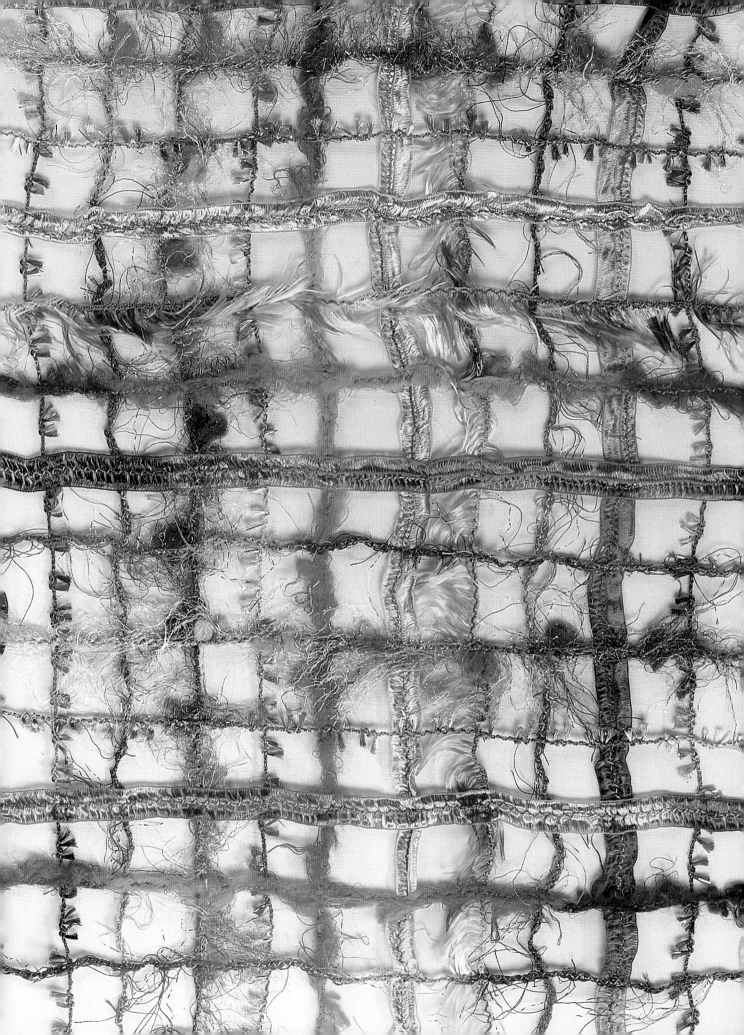

ribbon netting

Take advantage of the gorgeous trim, ribbon, and yarn available today and create a work of art.

Stitch a delicate, airy network of colorful, textural fibers to make a chic accessory or quick gift. Sew the ribbon netting to fabric to add a textural aspect, or use the trim to make an impressive wall hanging. Start with a water-soluble stabilizer, sew the trim or ribbon to it, and then dissolve the stabilizer away. You may find this addictive!

materials and tools

Water-soluble stabilizer: Sulky Super Solvy

Washable ribbon

Cotton thread: 40 or 50 weight

Sewing machine

Permanent marker (optional)

Straight pins

Container with water to dissolve stabilizer

Terry towel

ribbon netting

Grab your favorite ribbon and trim and in just a few **short steps, construct a colorful scarf or** a work of art...or maybe they're one and the same!

1

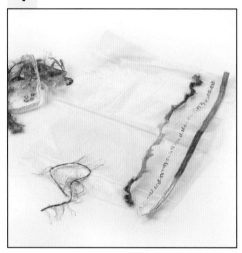

Cut two pieces of stabilizer slightly larger than the planned size of your finished project. Cut several pieces of ribbon the length of the stabilizer.

2

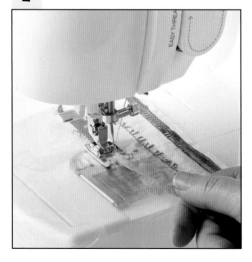

Place a ribbon parallel to the edge of one piece of stabilizer. Sew down the middle of the ribbon with a narrow zigzag stitch, backstitching the ends. Continue to add ribbons, spacing them about 1" (2.5 cm) apart, until the stabilizer is covered. The ribbons do not need to be perfectly straight, but draw guidelines on the stabilizer with a permanent marker, if you like.

3

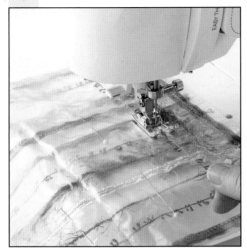

Lay the second piece of stabilizer on top of the first piece and pin in place. Sew additional ribbons perpendicular to those forming the first layer and backstitch at the ends.

4

Soak the piece in warm water to dissolve the stabilizer. If you feel any stickiness, soak again in clean water. Any remaining stabilizer will make the netting stiff. Reshape on a terry towel to dry.

Susan Suggests

Make a scarf using the netting technique. Cut a 20" x 60" (50.8 x 152.4 cm) piece of stabilizer. Cut eight to twelve pieces of ribbon 72" (183 cm) long. Sew the ribbons lengthwise over one-half of the stabilizer, letting an extra 6" (15.2 cm) hang off both ends to form fringe. Fold the stabilizer over the ribbons. Cut approximately 60 pieces of ribbon 10" (25.4 cm) long and sew them perpendicular to those forming the first layer, and backstitch at the ends. Dissolve the stabilizer.

Susan Stein 2008

no-sew matted assemblage

Misty Fuse is a fusible web that is very sheer and not sticky, so you can layer up netting, lace, or other open weave fabrics with ease.

The fusible web will not come up through the holes or stiffen the fabric. Collect mementos of an event or highlight a favorite fabric motif, even trap dried materials under netting for an unusual look.

materials and tools

8½" by 11" (21.5 x 28 cm) piece of sheer fabric such as tulle, bridal netting, or a chiffon scarf

inkjet photo transfer fabric sheets or 8½" by 11" (21.5 x 28 cm) piece of fabric for background

photo on the computer or an 8" by 10" (20 x 25.5 cm) print (optional)

inkjet copier or computer printer (optional)

cheesecloth colored with dye or paint

ribbons or trims

buttons, ticket stubs, or other mementos (optional)

silk or dried flowers, leaves, or grass (optional)

cut-outs from printed fabric (optional)

two 8½" by 11" (21.5 x 28 cm) pieces of Misty Fuse fusible web

cooking parchment

clear drying fabric glue

11" by 14" (28 x 35.5 cm) precut mat with an opening approximately 8" by 10" (20 x 25.5 cm)

8½" by 11" (21.5 x 28 cm) piece of batting

cardboard cut slightly larger than the assemblage

no-sew matted assemblage

1

Print an 8" by 10" (20 x 25.5 cm) photo onto fabric on the computer or copier and lay aside to dry. Or you can cut a 8½" x 11" (21.5 x 28 cm) piece of fabric for your background. Cut a piece of Misty Fuse the same size. Iron the Misty Fuse on top of the background or photo, using parchment paper over the top to protect the iron.

Note: It's always a good idea to put a piece of cooking parchment under the background in case some fusible web goes beyond the edges.

2

Lay the mat over the background to determine how much area you have to cover. Most mats have openings less than a full 8" by 10" (20 x 25.5 cm). Arrange ribbons or trims over the Misty Fuse. Try to keep them as flat as possible. Lay on pieces of colored cheesecloth.

3

Arrange cut-out fabric motifs, dried materials, ticket stubs, commemorative buttons, award ribbons, silk flowers, etc., on top of the layers.

4

Lay a second piece of Misty Fuse over the assemblage and then cover the layers with tulle, netting, or chiffon. Cover with cooking parchment and iron to secure all the elements.

Continued

no-sew matted assemblage (continued)

5

Add trims or other elements to the top of the sheer layer with fabric glue if you wish. Make sure you check the opening in your mat before gluing anything down.

6

Back the assemblage with batting so it will round out the edges when you add the mat. If you want to, you can add hand stitching to accent certain elements or give texture, sewing through the assemblage and the batting.

7

Run a bead of glue around the back side of the mat opening. Place the mat carefully over the top of the assemblage and press down firmly. Place books over the top to weigh down the mat while the glue is drying.

8

Glue the cardboard on the back of the mat to cover and support the assemblage. Weigh the mat down with books until the glue dries. You can decorate the mat to coordinate with the assemblage, and be sure to sign your artwork.

Susan Suggests

Place the matted assemblage in a frame, possibly with a second mat added to set the artwork away from the glass or set a grouping of matted pieces without frames on a long, narrow shelf along with coordinating accessories.

collage with fabric

Collage has been done with paper for many years. Here we adapt it to fabric to create texture and dimension.

Most of the projects in this book involve fun and spontaneous techniques, so why not forgo the exact seam allowances, perfect corners, and precise measurements that normally make up a wall hanging and let yourself play. Collect trim, fabrics, beads, buttons, embellishments, orphan quilt blocks, fibers, and ribbon. Toss in the new techniques you've discovered in *The Complete Fabric Artist's Workshop*, and create a piece that tells your story!

materials and tools

Background fabric

Accent fabrics, blocks, screen prints, embroidered hankies

Trim, silk flowers and leaves, ribbon to coordinate with the fabrics

Batting: fusible, thin

Backing fabric

Iron

Glue stick or basting glue

Sewing machine

Thread

Buttons, beads, charms

collage with fabric

A project that takes us back to hunting and gathering—and helps use up the bits of ephemera we all have stashed away!

1

Select a background fabric for your collage. From your stash, gather trim, accent fabrics, buttons, anything that will coordinate with your background fabric and the theme you've chosen for the piece.

2

Cut a piece of background fabric and a piece of batting to 8½" x 11" (21.6 x 27.9 cm). Cut a backing fabric to 9½" x 12" (24.1 x 30.5 cm). Layer the background fabric (right side out), batting, and the backing fabric (right side out), and fuse them together with an iron, following the batting manufacturer's instructions.

3

Cut small pieces of accent fabrics, ribbon, and trim, and glue-baste them onto the background fabric, auditioning everything that might work. Relate elements to each other by overlapping them or connecting them with a ribbon or trim. If you have a digital camera, take photographs of different arrangements before you decide on one. Stitch around the edges or through the centers of the elements, through the batting and backing.

4

Press the extra backing fabric around to the top. Glue-baste the turned fabric to the journal page top to create a binding, folding in the corners as you go. Topstitch or satin stitch the edge of the binding. Hand sew beads, buttons, and charms onto the background fabric through all the layers.

Note: Sunprinted leaves by Diane Bartels.

Susan Suggests

For even more freedom, try using quilt-as-you-go methods. Of course, you will want to make a larger piece after doing this journal page, and a fat quarter would be a good size for a larger background. You can either finish your project at that size or add borders or other pieces later.

collaged wall hanging

Quilts are becoming more and more personal, not just in color selection and labeling, but also in composition.

Collage allows us to collect all sorts of elements and embellishments that convey a message or mood and then sew them onto a small background piece using relaxed methods of construction.

Celebrate an event, portray an emotion, remember a vacation, or just enjoy using your favorite images. Then display your collage on the wall where it will be enjoyed daily. Start collecting!

materials and tools

- prints: screen prints, sun prints, rubber-stamped images on fabric
- fabric: odd blocks, hankies, special cuts of print fabric, accent fabrics
- embellishments: buttons, skeleton leaves, feathers, shells, ribbons, yarns to couch, lace, trims such as "eyelash"
- beads, including fabric beads (see page 27)
- photo transfers on fabric
- background fabric: fat quarter (approximately 18" x 22" [45.5 x 56 cm])
- iron
- rotary cutter, acrylic ruler, and mat
- border/binding fabric: ⅝ yd. (0.6 m)

- fusible batting
- backing fabric: ¾ yd. (0.7 m)
- black fabric
- scissors
- pins
- threads: decorative, invisible, beading if using glass beads
- sewing machine
- hand-sewing needle
- clear-drying fabric glue
- permanent marking pen
- inkjet copy machine

collaged wall hanging

1

Collect orphan quilt blocks, small sun prints and screen prints, rubber-stamped images, ribbons, lace, buttons, beads, photos transferred to fabric, skeleton leaves, yarns, etc. that coordinate in theme, color, or mood. Put them up on the design wall with possible choices for background fabric.

2

Press and straighten the background fabric. For the border, cut three 3" (7.6 cm)-wide strips using a rotary cutter, ruler, and mat. Cut 25" x 29" (63.6 x 73.5 cm) pieces of batting and backing fabric. Cut 2" (5 cm)-wide strips of binding fabric.

3

Lay the backing fabric on the batting, and fuse together with steam. Turn over and steam-fuse the background fabric in the center of the batting. The borders will be added later. Place the quilt sandwich on the design wall.

4

Arrange the larger elements such as the screen prints, sun prints, old quilt blocks, etc. on the background. To make these items pop out visually, center them over black fabric cut ½" (1.3 cm) larger. Remember the art theory that odd numbers look better than even numbers. Vary the sizes and shapes of your elements. Use diagonal lines and on-point placement for interest. Keep in mind that you will be adding more embellishments, so don't fill every space. Pin the elements in place.

Continued

collaged wall hanging (continued)

5

Connect the larger elements with ribbons, yarn, or other directional items. You want to unify all the various parts of the collage, carrying the viewer's eye around the piece and holding her interest. Some of the ribbons or yarns can go under the larger units and some can go over the sides or edges. Pin everything in place.

6

Choose threads that coordinate or contrast with the parts of the collage. Stitch ⅛" (3 mm) in from the edges of the larger units, appliquéing and quilting in one operation. Stitch down both sides or down the middle of the ribbons. Stitching down the middle will raise the edges and give more dimension. Stitch over the yarns with a zigzag stitch and invisible thread.

7

Cut one strip of border fabric in half, and trim it to the exact horizontal size of your background piece. Place the top and bottom border strips right sides together with the background fabric and sew through all the layers with a ¼" (6 mm) seam. Open up the border strips and steam to the batting. Sew the side borders on in the same way.

8

Add smaller embellishments such as cut squares or triangles, leaves, or appliqués, extending them onto the borders, if desired. Sew around the edges of each unit or use detail stitching to attach them, such as using veins in a leaf to sew it down instead of edge stitching. Trim and bind the edges of the wall hanging and add a casing to the back for hanging. Hand-sew or glue fragile or hard elements such as skeleton leaves, beads, buttons, and feathers. Sign and date the wall hanging with a permanent pen.

Susan Suggests

Fresh flowers or three-dimensional items such as rocks or shells can't be stitched to your collage, but you can still include them. Lay them directly on an inkjet copy machine, print a fabric sheet, and add the print to your collage instead.

Influences
by Doroth Mayer

Photo transfer, rust-dyeing.

Fantasy Vine
by Susan Stein

More than twenty different
techniques on leaves.

Hot & Spicy
by Susan Stein

Collage, ribbon netting.

StarBuilder Mariner's Compass
by Laura Murray

Paintstiked and fused using Laura's new rubbing tools.

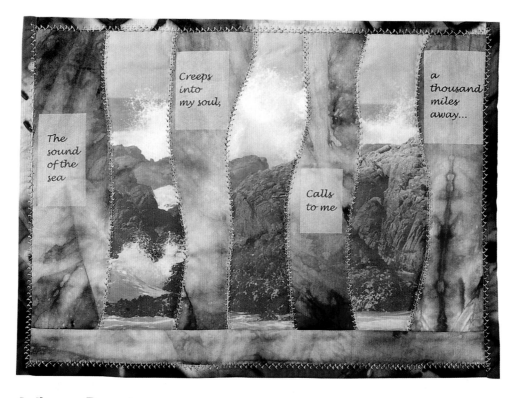

Asilomar Reverie
by Susan Stein
Photo transfer.

Dye-na-Flow Sampler
by Susan Stein

Nine different Dye-na-Flow painting techniques.

Feather Discharge
by Sue Kelly

Discharge and paint.

Leaf Montage
by Susan Stein

Rubber stamping, screen printing, and sun printing
by Diane Bartels; shibori dyeing by Deb Lunn;
overdyed background by Wendy Richardson.

ing
by Tina Hughes

Various techniques.

Silk Surprises
by Susan Stein

Lasagna dyeing with Dye-na-Flow.

2008 Journal Class Samples
by Tina Hughes

Various techniques.

Orchid
by Elizabeth Palmer-Spilker

Photo transfer.

A pale dawn moon—
Furrows of the new-ploughed fields
white with frost.

MEMORIES HAIKU; JOURNAL PAGES   Tina Hughes

a poppy…
a field of poppies!
the hills blowing with poppies

MEMORIES HAIKU; JOURNAL PAGES   Tina Hughes

TURQUOISE AND COPPER; WALL HANGING   Susan Stein

DREAMING OF DRAGONFLIES; QUILT   Elizabeth Lanzatella

NORTHERN LIGHTS THROUGH PINE BOUGHS; JOURNAL PAGE
Elizabeth Palmer-Spilker

MEDITATION SCREEN   Susan Stein

CATCH A DREAM; WALL PANEL   Susan Stein

CONTEMPORARY TECHNIQUES, TRADITIONAL CONCEPTS; QUILT
Joyce Kvaas

FLOATING LEAVES; WALL HANGING   Susan Stein

COPPER, LIGHT AND SHADOW; WALL HANGING   Susan Stein

MARKINGS IN THE ROCKS; COLLAGE   Susan Stein

resources

Art Supplies

www.joggles.com
www.dickblick.com
www.artquiltingsupplies.com
www.quiltingarts.com

Hand-dyed fabrics, organza, and twill tape

Wendy Richardson, www.qtstudio.com

Hand-dyed fabric bundles

www.cherrywoodfabrics.com

Paint, photo-transfer paper, prepared-for-dyeing fabrics, textile medium, books, Jacquard Discharge Paste, Anti-Chlor, dyes and chemicals, and information online

www.dharmatrading.com

Painting books, classes, and rubber stamps

Sherrill Kahn, www.impressmenow.com

Paintstiks, stencil brushes, original rubbing plates

Cedar Canyon Textiles
www.cedarcanyontextiles.com

Photo-transfer paper

www.transferartist.com

Print paste SH, dye, Synthrapol, soda ash, urea, and Pebeo Setacolor paints and medium

www.prochemicalanddye.com

Printed images

Ready to Use North American Indian Motifs, Dover Publications, 1996

ReVisions Stencils by Diane Ericson

www.dianeericson.com

Rust-dyeing supplies and instructions

www.rust-tex.com

Silk fabric and scarves

www.thaisilks.com
800-722-7455

Silk roving

www.treenwaysilks.com

Stencils, paint sticks, foil for fabric, and foil adhesive

www.lauramurraydesigns.com

Thermofax screens

Nancy Mambi, email address: nancymambi@comcast.net

acknowledgments

Thanks to so many wonderful friends—Diane Bartels, Laura Murray, Mary Johnson, Wendy Richardson, Shelly Stokes, Elizabeth Palmer-Spilker, and Sue Kelly—who have opened my eyes to the joys of playing with fabric in new ways; to students who have taught me a lot more than I have taught them; to my husband, John, who encourages me always; and to the staff at Creative Publishing international, who have always believed in me.

about the author

Susan Stein started quilting in 1977 and has delighted in getting other people obsessed with quilting and surface design ever since. This former president and show chairman for Minnesota Quilters was named Minnesota Quilter of the Year in 2003. An energetic and passionate quilter, Susan has shared her talents as the author of four books and as a contributing author to numerous others. She has taught many classes in Minnesota and around the country. Many of the hundreds of quilts produced by her hands serve as wall hangings, publication pieces, and store samples, while others are on public display or in personal use.

index